ACHIEVING A MEANINGFUL RETIREMENT

A Common-sense Approach to Planning for Retirement and Beyond

by

Clarice Santa

"Because many people now live into their 80's and often 90's, retirement could span one third or more of our lives. That is certainly worth being prepared for."

authorHOUSE®

AuthorHouse™
1663 Liberty Drive, Suite 200
Bloomington, IN 47403
www.authorhouse.com
Phone: 1-800-839-8640

First published by AuthorHouse 1/16/2008

ISBN: 978-1-4343-2024-7 (sc)

Library of Congress Control Number: 2007904827

Printed in the United States of America
Bloomington, Indiana

This book is printed on acid-free paper.

Foreword

I met Clarice more than thirty years ago when we were both studying to be teachers. Careers, marriage, children and family life followed in due course. Our lives became filled with demands and challenges, joys and sorrows, time crunching and busyness, yet Clarice still managed to keep thoughts of a time when life would be different in mind. With the publication of her book, *Achieving a Meaningful Retirement*, it is my pleasure to say that the wisdom of her life experiences and the common sense of her preparation for the future will now be shared.

As I began turning the pages of her work, I realized that it was written for somebody just like me. By extension, that would mean that it would appeal to people nearing, at, or even in retirement. Once I completed the book, however, I became aware that *Achieving a Meaningful Retirement* would also be a worthwhile read for a much broader audience. Although most subjects are geared to retirees, people with retired friends and family would find the book to be a valuable source of information. Additionally, some chapters would interest all readers who like to travel or prepare healthy meals, for example. Since the book examines many important life issues, it speaks to a universal readership.

Achieving a Meaningful Retirement is easy to read, and it is divided into chapters for quick referencing. Each section is not only informative but also entertaining as well due to Clarice's use of personal experiences. It is a valuable book filled with references and planning guides, knowledge and understanding, and explanations and descriptions of what your future could become. Congratulations on your accomplishment of *Achieving a Meaningful Retirement*, Clarice.

Pat Wiebe

To retirees, past, present and future

Acknowledgements

To recognize all of the people that should be acknowledged is an impossible task. In conversations over the years, many stories that have been shared with me remained in my memory. In most instances, I remember the story but not the teller. Everyone's help and insights have been valuable and greatly appreciated.

My ideas about retirement took shape over the course of my life. It is a part of my personality. The need to be prepared for everything that occurs in my life is ever present, and retirement was no exception.

My own experiences, along with those of my grandparents and parents, have been shaped into a multitude of suggestions about preparing for retirement.

I am grateful for the positive encouragement of my family. My husband has given me ongoing support. My daughter and son-in-law edited my first draft and gave me ideas for improving my manuscript. My son and my daughter assisted me with technology that sometimes puzzles me. Thanks to all of them for their input into the final draft, for their sense of humor and for their love.

When I was looking for elusive information, I was assisted by Wendy Dickout, Linda Flaman, and Erna Goertzen.

Edith Heim, a friend, skillfully created my Website.

Jim Asplund, a fellow retired teacher, edited my revised manuscript. Jim shares my interest in local history, and is a published author and friend.

Pat Wiebe, a long time acquaintance and an English teacher, did what English teachers do best. She defended the integrity of the English language and its correct usage. Her patience and dedication was greatly appreciated.

Table of Contents

Introduction

A long time curiosity of mine was recently made personal when I retired from a career in teaching. I have always been very interested in how others handle aging and retirement.

I have come to believe that we all deserve to spend our retirement years with as much fulfillment, happiness, and peace of mind as we are capable of creating for ourselves.

Let's start with the premise that the above goals are best achieved by planning for retirement in a proactive way. If you have avoided formulating your plan until after retirement, it is not too late. However, it may be more difficult to incorporate all the changes that will be required in a short period of time. After reading this book, my hope is that you will have some ideas about where to start.

To be successful at anything, you must begin with a plan. The contents of your retirement plan should be flexible enough to allow for changes and growth. Having this outline prevents you from feeling disconnected or ungrounded. During your working years you constantly plan to meet your commitments, to budget your time wisely and to give yourself a sense of direction. In order to be successful at achieving balance, your life needs structure.

While you are working, not having to plan every aspect of your life sounds enticing, and enjoying spur-of-the-moment choices is enjoyable for short periods of time. This unstructured approach is renewing, but weekends and vacations end, and the rest of your life continues. In retirement, the unstructured portion of your time may increase in size or it may not. However, the need for balance will not change. Your challenge is to use your newly gained flexibility and choices to make your life fulfilling and rewarding. Having structure helps us meet that challenge.

The ideas for coping with change and living a very full happy retirement found in this book may inspire and benefit you.

When to begin making plans and living them is the question. For each of you, that may differ slightly. Should you start one year, two years, five years, ten years or twenty years before you retire? All of the above are correct when applied to various aspects of your lives.

When considering the content of your retirement agenda you can look at it as having three components. Part one should be to continue with your choice of established hobbies, interests and good lifestyle habits. Part two should consist of changes to those areas of your lifestyle that will promote longevity and improved health. In part three, you should incorporate activities that you have been unable to participate in while you were working. You may attempt to start your participation in some of these activities before you actually stop work. By making changes gradually, the transition into retirement will be much easier.

I do not have all the answers to questions that you may have, and only parts of this book may apply to you. I shall, however, be pleased if I can assist you in the planning of your personal journey through retirement.

Chapter One

Why Plan Ahead?

We plan to give ourselves a sense of direction and structure. As working adults, to varying degrees, we try to approach our lives in a manner that facilitates a sense of achievement. We feel most satisfaction when we are accomplishing our goals or doing what we want to do. In looking ahead to retirement, we may ask this question: What possibilities does the final 1/3 of my life hold? Exploring a multitude of possibilities and preparing a blueprint containing our choices should allow us to continue experiencing a sense of satisfaction and achievement.

By the nature of the very word, planning implies that you are looking at a variety of possibilities, weighing them one against the other and then making choices. Research at some level is necessary. If you are redecorating your bathroom, you would visit supply stores to become aware of your options; you may bring samples home to compare, or look through catalogs for ideas. If a European holiday is what you are looking forward to, your research would most likely include books, the Internet, travel magazines or a travel agent. You must decide what research is appropriate for your needs. Friends or family are ones with whom you share your excitement, but for reliable information they would only be a start.

The planning that you do well before your last day on the job will, to some degree, determine how successfully you move from your last day at work to the rest of your life. There are many aspects of your life to which you could apply preplanning. Here is one example from my life. Five years prior to my last day as a teacher, I decided that I wanted to stay physically fit after I retired. For my fiftieth birthday I asked my husband for a treadmill. For me that was a commitment. For the five years that followed, I tried several walking routines. The most successful one was in place well in advance of my retirement. As the last day of my career approached, the most important aspect of my physical fitness program did not require change. I started the first day of my official retirement with a brisk four-mile walk.

During all the years that you spend working outside the home, one of the requirements is that you be efficient. After retirement you will most likely continue to feel the need to be efficient and to enjoy the positive rewards of accomplishments. The change now is that your goals are self-planned and self-imposed. Your plans will, to a much greater degree, reflect what *you* want to do.

Planning in time blocks

Planning should be done at a variety of levels. These levels are daily, weekly, monthly, seasonally, yearly, in groups of years, such as in the next two years, by the time I turn sixty and so on.

You need to have an attitude of flexibility about your plans. If you decide ahead of time that flexibility is good, then when something interesting or unexpected comes up, you will not feel torn. You can postpone an item in your plan to another day, week, month, or year. You may even want to re-evaluate and eliminate that item altogether.

Daily

I find a daily plan or timetable to be useful. This plan need not necessarily be written on paper, although it can be if you choose. Each morning or the evening before, I make a rough one, usually as mental notes. My considerations include daily living routines, joint goals (with my husband), and personal goals and challenges.

I like to divide my day into blocks of time. A fairly typical day for me starts out with a four-hour segment.

As my day progresses, the size of the segments may change. Here is one example:

7:00-11:00… This time is used for personal care, reading the paper, eating breakfast, walking, making needed phone calls, and doing chores that can't wait.

11:00-3:00… This time is usually set aside for creativity or for running errands if needed. By creativity I mean writing, or working on a craft or hobby. About a half hour is used for lunch, and if needed, a cat nap of anywhere from five to ten minutes is taken.

3:00-6:30… I read for about one hour, watch one hour of TV, prepare and eat the evening meal, and clean up.

6:30-10:00… Activities in this time slot vary greatly. My choices may be playing nine holes of golf, curling, playing bridge, enjoying a hobby, seeing a movie, cleaning something, taking a walk, gardening or just relaxing.

Note: In the summer, golf may be slotted into any time period. It is often my priority.

Your own personal plan should include the things that are important to you and those that you share with your significant other. Blocks of time most suited to you may vary greatly from someone else's blocks of time.

Weekly

My weekly plans consist of a list that sits on the kitchen counter. The items that appear on the list are numbered, and I use a highlighter to cross off the completed ones. This list helps me sort things out in my head, and it acts as a reminder. As I check items off, I feel a sense of accomplishment. The items that I do not get around to are either transferred to next week's list or deleted if they have lost their importance.

For those who have always laughed at list makers, this may be a good time to recognize the value of this exercise. Although your memory should continue to be challenged, having a list may save time and the embarrassment of forgetting. As my husband and I age, we are sometimes frustrated by something we have forgotten. At other times it gives us a good reason to laugh at ourselves and to reinforce the belief that writing it down would have saved us some frustration. We often bet a quarter on differing opinions or on outcomes of one thing or another, such as sporting events. It can be an opportunity for a shared laugh when we realize that neither of us remembers what the bet was.

Monthly or seasonally

Monthly or seasonal plans could be dealt with in a fashion similar to a weekly plan. They could and should be revised as the need arises. If you have a spouse or a partner, some of your long-range plans can and should include joint goals and perhaps challenges. If both of you would like to learn how to play tennis, you may want to take lessons at the same time. By doing that, you are developing an activity that you can participate in together. Hopefully you can strike a balance of things that you do in your personal time with things that the two of you do together. I feel that having personal time improves your together time.

In summary, I truly believe that although planning for one's retirement in the long and short term is vital, flexibility is equally important and is a component that makes us cherish our newly gained freedom.

Chapter Two

Taking Care of Your Physical and Mental Health

It is difficult to separate physical and mental health, since they work together. There is no universal plan of action for *taking care* that works for everyone equally. You must each learn what your choices are. When making lifestyle choices that may include changes, you must consider your individual circumstances and present state of health and fitness. The changes that you make will hopefully lead to an improved lifestyle, one that is suitable for your upcoming or present retirement. Two things that are **not** choices, in my opinion, are having yearly check-ups by your doctor and taking medication when *necessary.*

As much as possible, living a healthy life style should be practiced by all. By that I mean limiting the drinking of alcoholic beverages, refraining from smoking, exercising regularly, eating foods that provide nutrients which promote better health, and keeping our minds active. Having a spiritual component in our lives can be very comforting. It gives me peace of mind, and in that way contributes to my better health.

I believe in the use of vitamins and some supplements. You can obtain information as a basis to formulate your opinions from doctors who promote preventative medicine. You may also want to read books and health magazines that base their articles on documented research. Your doctor may help you decide which vitamins and supplements may benefit you.

Outside the two choices that I consider essential, you have many choices to make. I shall dedicate separate chapters to diet or healthy eating, exercise, hobbies and interests.

The remainder of this chapter shall be devoted to ideas that may contribute to good mental health. Most of these ideas are directed to those who are already in retirement; however, they may be useful to any age group.

Personal Choices
Goal setting

We *need* to set **goals** for ourselves. Having a purpose to our day makes us look forward to it. These goals should be short and long-term.

An example of a *short-term daily goal* may be to clean a particular closet or have a quiet lunch with one of the grandchildren. An example of a *short-term goal for the week* may be to re-pot some plants. A weekly goal may involve some pre-planning such as buying the necessary soil or gloves, or waiting for a sunny day.

A longer goal, although not really a long-term goal, may be to walk 32 miles this month. That mileage can be what ever distance you choose. The important part is that you spent time considering a goal and making a commitment to achieving it.

A *seasonal goal* can be very useful and rewarding when completed. Last spring my goal was to plant a rose garden and to rearrange my rock garden by transplanting the plants that were already there. Neither of these was a one or two day job. The changes required planning, execution and on- going maintenance.

Some examples of *long-term goals* are preparing for a trip later in the year, planning for a family reunion, telephoning lost acquaintances, redecorating a room and on and on. Long-term goals often, if not always, involve budgeting, extensive organization and other people. This coordination and execution takes time.

Challenges

Not to be confused with goals are **challenges**. These are necessary to keep our minds active, to give us a sense of self worth and to achieve a great deal of satisfaction. We all need them. We should keep in mind that our requirements for challenges are determined by our interests, our finances and our personal capabilities.

Cleaning a closet (goal), something that you know you can accomplish with ease, can be turned into a challenge. You may be challenged to create space where none exists. This would require you to draw a plan and possibly learn and apply some carpentry skills.

You can easily tell that challenges can also be goals, but goals are not necessarily challenges.

My present challenge is writing this book and getting it published. It is also one of my long-term goals. During my career as a teacher, composing, organizing, planning, writing, editing, and creating were a large part of what I did. I am now using those skills to challenge myself.

You need to choose your challenges carefully. You want to make choices that have the potential for success. Fear of failure should not be allowed to dictate the choice. Fear of failing as I write this book is ever present. However, I thought that my chance of succeeding was reasonable. The skills that I cultivated as a teacher, and my resolve and willingness to invest the time that would be required were strong motivators.

An example of a poor choice for me would be to challenge myself to win a prestigious golf tournament. I am a golfer, or more accurately, I am a social golfer. To begin with, I do not possess the skills to win a tournament; at my age, learning or relearning the necessary skills would probably be close to, if not impossible, and I do not have the inner motivation to try. This choice would be a formula for failure.

So where should you start? First you should make an inventory of skills and knowledge that you possess and then devise a challenge that will build on those. You could also choose a challenge by pursuing something that interested you in the past but was not pursued because you had insufficient time, energy or resources. You may need to take a course or arrange for practice. Give yourself time to become skilled or sufficiently comfortable to proceed. Know that you may never be good at this choice, but the experience you gain and the satisfaction you feel in trying something new are valuable. Examples of challenges in this category may be ballroom dancing, swimming, carpentry, or quilting, to name a few.

My mother learned to drive a car in her mid sixties. It was a challenge that was difficult to perfect at that age. Her new skill increased her independence and gave her the satisfaction of conquering a new challenge.

Setting priorities

By the time you retire from your life's work and start your new life, you and your spouse or partner should have a workable understanding about what you want to do in your together time. General guidelines should be put in place. For my husband and me, travel has a high priority. Camping and other outdoor pursuits may be priorities for others.

Be flexible enough to change if you both discover that changes are needed. It's easier to start with some plans and then make changes than it is to have no starting place at all.

A couple that I know recently retired together at age sixty. He was elated because he thought they would spend every possible moment at their lakeside cabin away from their permanent residence. She went along with this arrangement for a while, but soon became weary of being away from what she considered home. A solution had to be found. Perhaps a compromise. What they failed to do initially was to formulate a plan which kept both of their needs in mind.

In Partnership with Physical Health
Use of aids

In order to maintain your sense of well-being, you may need to help yourselves with physical problems you encounter.

If a hearing aid is needed, you should get one. After all, if you were having problems with your vision, you would not think of managing without glasses. The same holds true for helping yourself hear better.

A very useful aid that assists me is a large and powerful magnifying glass. There are instances when small print is difficult to read, even when wearing glasses. When I first brought the magnifying glass to work and used it in the staff room, I heard a snicker or two (good-natured of course). I hope that those who snickered remember how I solved my problem when it eventually becomes their problem. Improving your ability to interact with your environment by using artificial aids is far superior to submitting to powerlessness.

Sleep

At this point in your lives you need your sleep just as much as you always have. It may be more difficult to get that sleep all at one time, such as during the night. A variety of issues such as weaker bladders, aching joints, aching backs or menopause may be getting in the way.

Get in the habit of making every effort to have a better sleep, and more of it. If you find yourself not getting sufficient rest, there may be more that you can do.

Over time I have tried many strategies. Here are some that have worked to varying degrees of success for my friends and for me:

- Keep regular hours for bedtime and for getting up in the morning.

- Drink plenty of liquids in the earlier part of the day and none at all for the last two to three hours before bedtime.

- Avoid coffee and other liquids or foods that contain caffeine, later than four or five in the afternoon.

- Exercise regularly.

- Avoid alcoholic beverages before bedtime.

- Get up if you are unable to fall asleep, and read, take a warm-to-hot bath, or do something quiet until you feel sleepy.

- Take one or two short catnaps during the day. You can train yourself to have five to ten minute naps. Avoid napping later than about three o'clock, since later naps may interfere with the quality of your night sleep.

- Sleep in a bed that satisfies requirements for comfort. That will most likely be a firm bed with good head support. It may also mean having special support, such as an extra pillow, for an arm or between the knees. Some people have an allergy to feathers, and must avoid them. Others have the best sleep on a feather pillow.

- Drink a small warm glass of milk just before turning in for the night.

- Make an extra effort to eliminate all light sources including digital clocks.

Partners

You and your spouse or partner should look for signs of poor or failing health in the other. It may be the affected one who is ignoring signs and symptoms or he/she simply does not recognize gradual changes that are taking place. Many health problems or conditions may be treatable if they are tended to early. Talk to your doctor.

As you and your partner age, one of you may become more demanding of the other. Perhaps what is driving these demands may be the symptom of a condition that needs medical attention. Consult your doctor. If you discover that there is a real need for this increased demand on your attention, give your partner the time needed. You may require a surrogate caregiver or support person, as you will no doubt need time outs in order to keep a balanced perspective. Don't expect yourself to be a super person. Very few of us can manage these demands over an extended period of time.

General Suggestions
Staying informed

You should take steps to stay grounded and informed about what is happening in your world near and far. To avoid any feelings of confusion, you should orient yourself with time of day, day of the week, and approximate temperature, and then discover what is happening in your community and the world. That knowledge can be gained by reading both your community newspaper and one that covers national and world news. You can also stay in touch by watching the TV news, listening to the radio or reading the news on the Internet. I often choose reading, since reading is a very good way to exercise my mind.

Daily routines

Helping yourselves remember the routines of everyday living is very important. Recalling things such as appointments, medication, and important dates could be problematic to some at a fairly early age, and to most of us as time goes on. A prominently placed calendar with large spaces to write in can serve as a reminder. You should make a point of jotting down all appointments as soon as you make them. The same calendar can be used for other dates to remember, such as birthdays. On the first day of every month (or thereabout) you should update your calendar for that month. The second option is to keep a sheet of paper and pencil on your counter or desk. Record all important dates and appointments for a chosen period of time. The paper must be kept in a place where it is easily accessible in the midst of your daily routines.

Where medications are concerned, a very simple but effective memory aid is to have a small calendar and a pen or pencil with the medications. Checking the date off is *part of the routine* of taking them. You can also buy a small container with days of the week clearly marked on it. These are commercially made specifically for the purpose of keeping yourself organized. Taking medications the same time of day every day helps you remember them.

With a conscious effort, you can train yourself until the routine becomes a habit.

That routine is usually broken when you travel. A suggestion for dealing with that will be addressed later.

Independent time

During your years of working outside the home, you spent a good number of your waking hours away from your spouse or partner. During that time, you were creative, exercised social skills and generally stayed mentally active. Although the amount of time away from your spouse or partner may change in retirement, the need for having personal time does not. It is not necessary to be in a different building to achieve having personal time. You need to create your own little nook where you enjoy your independence doing something of your choice. It is important that both individuals understand that need for independent time and respect it.

Change of pace

I found that in my last five years of formal work, I started to pace myself in almost all my activities. I had to keep in mind that slowing down is normal as we age, and therefore guilt is not the feeling that we should associate with these changes. Changing the pace with which I handled daily routines and work contributed greatly to a successful transition into retirement.

The children grew up and left home. This meant that meal preparation was more relaxed, and there was a lesser need to stick to a rigid timetable. At a time when my energy level was higher, I had no difficulty continuing my hectic pace after I got home from work. I cooked well-balanced meals on a daily basis. However, as I neared age fifty, I sometimes needed a nap, or I just wanted to sit down and read the paper when I came home from work. In this way I re-energized before I went on with the remainder of the day and evening. This meant that changes needed to be made in daily routines. I began doing more food preparation during the weekend for use during weekdays. Meals such as hearty soups, casseroles, stews, lasagna, and roasts lent themselves well to reheating. The addition of vegetables and a salad to one of these main dishes provided a good meal with very little effort. What also helped was having a spouse who understood the necessity for these changes and supported them.

This kind of spousal support and understanding is important when applied to other aspects of everyday living as well.

Sharing the work load

Sharing the workload with your spouse or partner is important. Does this mean that each of you does exactly half of every job? It can, but in reality, for most of you this is not practical. Each of you has an

"I prefer to" list that you can share with your spouse. If he/she prefers to do the cooking and you prefer to clean up after, so be it. If you both dislike or really like doing one of those, then it makes sense to share the chore.

Another solution to the division of labor is a traditional approach where one partner does all the yard work and the other does everything in the house. Whatever formula you mutually arrive at for sharing the work should also be mutually acceptable.

Unacceptable workloads ratios are when one person "does it all" or when the workload is very unbalanced.

Agreeing to share the workload in the home is a good place to start. An agreement is, however, only the beginning. There needs to be a commitment by both partners to act. If one needs constant reminders, there will likely be resentment on both sides. A practical solution is to make a conscious effort to notice when the chore needs attention. Conscious effort over time becomes habit.

When you have retired do you have independent family members living with you. Unless these are young children or elderly parents, you need to be adept at asking and expecting your family to share in the care of the home and in the preparation of meals. After all, if they were on their own, they would be doing it all. You must not feel guilty about expecting this kind of cooperation. This is a time when **you** need some time for **your** personal goals and challenges. These goals and challenges may have been neglected while you contributed to the family as a working person. The amount of personal time needed will vary from person to person.

Hobbies and interests

One of the most important considerations when approaching retirement is to cultivate one or more hobbies and one or more interests. Many of us already have a number of both, and at retirement they provide continuity. Transition into retirement is much easier if everything in your life is not changing at the same time. Therefore, I believe that starting at least one hobby or pursuing at least one interest well before retirement is wise. The least amount of preparation for you is considering your options and making a commitment for post-retirement participation in your hobby and/or interest of choice.

Having said that, I also think that it is never too late to plan for and participate in a new hobby or interest. Planning and committing may be more difficult if left until later. A person who subjects him or herself to retirement without preparation is flirting with too many immediate changes. That scenario could be difficult to manage, even for those who handled many challenges at work with ease.

A story told to me recently is about a man who retired and used his new found time to rearrange all the closets, cabinets and cupboards in the home. He needed something to do and therefore plunged into a frenzy of rearranging and cleaning. On the surface he sounds like the man many of us would like to have in our house.

However, his activities were not appreciated by his spouse for a very good reason. She was the one who took care of those matters for more than thirty years, and he was interfering in her domain. This is only one example of what can happen if you suddenly find yourself with lots of time on your hands and no plan for its use. Some communication about the matter needed to take place. In a different home, the wife may have been only too happy to be rid of that chore. The point of this example is that communication must be forthright; the other person's feelings must be respected when a plan for your use of time is being formulated. In this case, he fulfilled a need of his own, and in the process, he totally disrespected hers.

Laughing with your partner

This is a time when you need to have an especially good relationship with your spouse or partner. Each must feel that he or she is not being singled out in situations that relate to aging. Laughing *with* each other about occurrences is much better than laughing *at* each other. In my home, my husband and I discovered that forgetting something is not a major issue if we can find a way to laugh about it. If it is of utmost importance that we remember, we write a reminder note, although we sometimes neglect to read it.

Physical appearance

No one's physical appearance is the same as it was in youth. Therefore you must strive to have an attitude of looking for and complimenting your partner about his/her present strengths.

Personal spending money

You must be very careful and sensitive with your partner's need for independence relating to money.

It should be understood by both of you that the size of the retirement purse may be different and usually smaller. The way to stretch and disperse what is in that new purse should be discussed and agreed upon.

This is a situation to be avoided. A couple retires at the same time. One partner then proceeds to take care of the couple's finances. The dispenser gives the other an "allowance" of X number of dollars per month. That sum may be viewed as inadequate. Discussion and communication are needed. A few minor adjustments may solve the problem. As far as I can tell, calling money you personally need, an "allowance", is somewhat demeaning, and the finances should **not** be referred to in this way.

Having one of the partners dispense the money to the other is another part of the problem. What usually happens is that the dispensing partner does not have the same restrictive attitude when it comes to his or her own "allowance".

Creating

Continue to **create.** This will help you to maintain an active, healthy mind and a positive outlook on your life.

You can create in the kitchen, on a sewing machine, by building furniture, through scrap booking, by writing and much more. The list is endless. What works best for me is making a list of possibilities and then choosing one.

Relaxing

Make time for relaxation. Newly retired people often find this difficult to do. You can start by not having a rigid plan for a Sunday. Watching your favorite sport in person or on TV may be relaxing to you. Reading all day in your pajamas may be relaxing to someone else. An extra long hike or bicycle ride may also be a choice. What is your choice?

Gradually make relaxation without guilt a part of every day.

Living single

If you are single and planning for retirement, your challenges are, for the most part, identical to those who are couples. In Chapter 8 the challenges and opportunities of living alone are discussed, at least in part.

What happens to you as you age is a mix of things that you can control with those that you cannot control. Each of you is living in a unique set of circumstances, and each of you is therefore challenged to address his/her retirement needs while keeping those circumstances in mind. How you manage your time, how you relate to those around you, and how you enrich your life in retirement, may contribute to your good mental health.

Chapter Three

Healthy Eating

We have all heard the saying, "we are what we eat". We know that what we eat has a cumulative effect on our health, our weight and influences our appearance. Other factors such as heredity play a large part as well. We have no control over heredity, but we can control our diets.

During our lifetime, what we eat has been influenced by many factors. When we are young we eat what we are fed. Our diets are determined by cultural influences, by the knowledge that our provider has about healthful foods and by our personal tastes. By the time we are adults, we have all those influences and one more. We now incorporate knowledge we have gained through reading, from school and from other sources.

When you were younger, your diets may not have consisted of healthy food choices, and your portion sizes may have been too large. The result may be that you carry too much weight and possibly experience related health issues. Another factor to consider is that as your body ages, your metabolic rate slows down. As you approach your late forties or fifties, you need to find the courage to make dietary choices that contribute to and help maintain a healthier body. For many, what is eaten and how much is eaten *must* change.

There are some basic changes to your diet that you can implement immediately. These are painless and may only result in minor taste differences.

1. Drink lots of **water**, and your body will not feel as hungry. The   recommended daily intake is at least 8 glasses. (All liquids that do not contain caffeine may be counted.)

2. Use **salt** sparingly. The only time I use salt is in soups, in pasta water, when blanching vegetables, in bread and in cakes. In soups I use salt for taste. Start with half of what you are accustomed to adding, and then work up in very small quantities if more is needed. In cakes, the claim is that salt enhances the taste of other ingredients. I have cut the quantity in half without noticing the difference. Where bread is concerned, you need to add the suggested

amount if you want the dough to rise properly. The pasta can be very bland if it is not salted and most of the salt remains in the water when the pasta is removed. The salt in the vegetable blanching liquid seems to set the color. When the vegetables are removed and immersed into cold water, the color and the crispness stay intact.

Salt can be left out of salads, raw vegetables, potatoes, cookies, or muffin dough. Other ingredients may provide the taste that is needed, especially in casseroles and other foods that are mixed. If you suspect that some salt is required, taste first and add in very small quantities.

3. Use **herbs** and **spices** to make food more palatable, and to allow you to reduce or eliminate the amount of salt used.

4. Use **skim milk** and **soy cheeses**. Two suggestions are ricotta and dry cottage cheese.

5. Use a **calorie- wise dressing**. The one that I use has only 6 calories per tablespoon.

Use only one quarter the amount of salad dressing that you would normally use.

When you are at a restaurant, you could order the dressing on the side and then dip your salad into it before each mouthful.

6. Add small amounts of **nuts** and **seed**s to salads.

7. Use **brown rice** or a mixture of different rices in place of white rice.

8. Eat bread that is made from **whole-wheat flour**. For added goodness, include *seeds* and *grains* such as sunflower, caraway, flax, wheat germ, millet, sesame and rolled oats.

9. Use one or more of the following for a taste that is irresistible*:* **garlic, onions, scallions, horseradish, ginger, prepared mixed seasonings, parsley, rosemary, basil, dill,** and **freshly ground pepper.** You may have some wonderful ideas of your own as well.

10. Eat oatmeal or porridge with some **fruit** for breakfast. Most fruits can be used.

11. Buy **pasta** that has been made from **whole-wheat flour**. It appears more like the white flour variety when it is cooked.

12. Get the **fats** that you need in your diet from *fish* (salmon, sardines and mackerel), *green leaves, olive oil, nuts, seeds* and *butter* in moderation. If you use margarine, the non-hydrogenated variety (without trans fats) is readily available now.

13. Substitute chocolate with **carob chips** in baking.

    If you find that this substitution is not suitable, use chocolate in smaller quantities. Also use **cocoa powder** in place of melted chocolate. Remember to decrease the amount of flour equal to the amount of cocoa powder added.

14. Treat yourself occasionally with a hard **candy**, one glass of **wine** or if you love **chocolate**, add a quarter cup to the banana loaf that you bake. Try adding small quantities to other recipes that you like.

15. Try new foods and food combinations.

    • Serve edamame as an appetizer. These are green soybeans. The pods must be removed before the beans are eaten.

- Serve chili in a bowl over a bed of rice. Slice a banana over the chili.

Note: When eating in a restaurant, portion sizes are usually too large. Order wisely and do not overeat.

Making healthier choices

A. Rather than remaking my total diet, I have successfully made changes in my ingredient selection without being too radical. You too can alter your favorite recipes in ways that will contribute to healthier eating and perhaps some weight loss. The changes that I suggest affect the texture of the food and possibly the appearance more than the taste.

I have been using most of these recipes for a long time, and many are in my memory rather than on paper. For that reason a source for the recipes shall not be included. You can find several examples of recipes that I have altered in APPENDIX A at the back of the book.

B. Another way to healthier eating is to choose recipes that do not need to be modified. They already contain foods that are better for building and maintaining good health. You may need to be a bit more adventurous than you are now. Becoming more knowledgeable about good choices and being open-minded about trying them are the keys to your success.

As you educate yourself about which foods are better for you, your new knowledge will assist you in locating healthier recipes. There are many sources for such recipes. I started from Canadian and American magazines for better health. Many books can also be obtained from health food stores, bookstores and libraries. A partial list of sources has been included at the back of this book in "Where to Find More Information", Chapter 15.

When choosing new recipes, consider these guidelines:

1. Does the recipe contain ingredients that you like? (At first you may need to try some new ingredients so that you can determine whether you like them or not.) An example of this is buckwheat groats. A recipe for a buckwheat casserole has been included in APPENDIX B.

2. Does the recipe contain ingredients that can be easily substituted with ones that are better for you? Examples of these are in recipe section APPENDIX A.

3. Do the foods in the recipe help you fulfill the requirements of your diet?

If you have a need to make changes in your cholesterol readings, you would make choices that avoid certain foods and have an abundance of foods that would promote healthier consequences.

Another example is choosing foods that help you maintain appropriate blood sugar levels if you are hypoglycemic. In order to keep your blood sugar from slipping too low too quickly, it is suggested that you eat foods with a low glycemic index number. "The factor, or GI, of foods affects the speed of conversion of foods to blood sugar (glucose). High value foods show a rapid response and subsequent increase in blood sugar. Conversely, complex carbohydrates and low GI range foods (those below 50) are absorbed slowly, causing a gradual rise in the blood sugar."

A snack of peanuts (glycemic number of 13) is a better snack than a chocolate bar (glycemic number of 68-76).

Source: *Eat to Beat Low Blood Sugar*, pages 46, 47

Complete reference is in Chapter 15 of this book.

Ask your doctor for more information.

4. Are the recipes a combination of ingredients that you should be including in your diet? Do they contain healthy fats, minerals, vitamins, fiber, proteins and complex carbohydrates?

5. Are you recognizing foods and ingredients that you should avoid or eat in smaller quantities? Avoid recipes that contain those ingredients. If you love and want to eat a particular food, treat yourself occasionally.

Some recipes that I would personally choose are in APPENDIX B at the back of the book. Each recipe contains at least one ingredient that is not commonly used. Each has ingredients with high fiber content, and each contains some ingredients with low glycemic numbers.

Note: To learn about foods that should be included in your diets, you can refer to *Canada's Food Guide* to healthy eating. This guide divides foods into four categories: grain products, vegetables and fruits, milk products, meats and alternatives. It lists the foods that each category is composed of and recommends the number of portions of each that you should be eating daily. It also gives shopping tips, discusses meal planning, suggests reading food labels, provides fast and easy meal ideas, and discusses smart snacking, eating out and counting servings.

You can access *Canada's Food Guide* at www.hc-sc.gc.ca. First choose the language you want, and then go to the navigation bar on the left and click on the **Food & Nutrition** link. On the

Food and Nutrition page, scroll down to *Canada's Food Guide*.

Other guides are available as well. One that I like to use was published in *Prevention* August, 2005, page 74. It is a "guide to the most common phytonutrients- plant components with the power to help prevent illnesses such as cancer and heart disease." Complete reference is in Chapter 15 of this book.

A comprehensive discussion about food and nutrition can be located in *Good Times,* March, 2007, page 20. The article is titled, "Eat Right for Your Age".

Another website that contains good suggestions for healthy eating is www.iVillage.com. Look for the **Total Health** link.

To determine how well you eat, start by making an honest assessment of your present food intake. Compare that with what you have learned about what your diet should include, and then proceed with making changes.

Congratulations if you are already there!

Chapter Four

Exercise

If someone told you that he or she exercised today, what picture would come to your mind? The only thing that I would know at this point is that the person was active in some way, moving body parts in ways that required effort.

Exercise levels fall into three categories. All exercise is mild, moderate or strenuous. The activity that you choose combined with your present physical condition will determine the category.

I like walking. My present level of walking is between three to four miles, three times per week at a rate of 15 minutes per mile. I consider this to be moderate exercise. If I reduced my rate to 25 minutes per mile and cut the number of miles to two, I would consider this mild exercise.

Let's compare this to someone who does not walk as exercise and whose fitness level is poor. Upon beginning to exercise, the person walks five blocks and comes home out of breath. That person is pushing his or her present conditioning level and is exercising more strenuously than I am. For that person, the exercise might even be considered strenuous.

In planning your exercise, you should include something that is considered a good cardio-vascular workout. You need to get your heart rate up for a sustained period of time. Your doctor can help you determine what exercise is appropriate for you. For most, swimming, fast walking outdoors or on a treadmill, riding bike outdoors or on a stationary bike indoors, running, mowing the lawn, snow shoveling and lifting weights would be considered a good workout. You may need to start at a lower level and work up slowly to a target level, as determined by you and your doctor.

You should make moving a variety of body parts a routine in your life. Create an exercise regime. It may be difficult at first. If you persist, your body will want you to exercise. You will feel best on the days that you do.

My exercise regime

My regime consists of what constitutes exercise in my life and occurs on a regular basis. It includes the following activities:

- Walking about 12-16 miles per week at my present rate of about 15 minutes per mile

- Golfing in the summer months three times per week

- Riding my bike in the evenings as often as I am able to for 15 minutes to ½ hour

- Completing 100 crunchies (a replacement for sit-ups) four to five times per week or 200-500 bicycles

- Completing additional exercises for my back the same time as crunchies

- Gardening in season about six hours per week

- Mowing the lawn occasionally

- Performing housework including cooking for about 10-12 hours weekly

- Fidgeting a lot

- Running when I use the stairs

- Executing yoga stretches for 15 minutes three or four times per week.

In addition to the above, I try to stay close to my suggested BMI (body mass index) weight. I do not always succeed. It is usually during the first part of January or after a vacation when I need to exercise more and eat less in order to return to my suggested range (or closer to it).

To find your BMI and learn more about it, go to: www.weightwatchers.com.

"Body Mass Index (BMI) is an assessment generally used by physicians and health experts to determine if a person is underweight, overweight or within the healthy weight range."

Another source of information about BMI is http://health.msn.com/dietfitness/articlepage.aspx?cp-documentid=100100526.

After reading the article in the above website, you will see that BMI does not appear to be a perfect measure, but it can be used as a guide.

Starting your exercise regime

Where should you start? Make an inventory of what you already do, and then add exercise if you are not doing enough. Try to add one activity at a time. If you add too many at once, the new activity level may be too difficult to maintain. Keep in mind that you may increase your exercise level by doing more of what you already do, by increasing the speed of exercise, or by adding new choices. For those of you who are just starting to increase your exercise levels from a relatively sedentary lifestyle, it is advisable to see a doctor before starting.

A good way to entice yourself to walk is to combine it with a creative activity. Many of my ideas for this book were conceived and pondered while I was walking. That is also where many of my Toastmasters speeches take shape.

A friend of mine told me that he bird watches, identifies plants, star gazes, thinks creatively and problem solves while walking.

You could choose to go to a gym for your fitness program. However, for a complete picture of what you do as exercise, you could add the many exercises that you already participate in at home and community.

Whatever you choose as your exercise, the important things are to keep your body moving, stretching, and bending, and your muscles challenged. Remember to include cardio vascular workouts in your exercise routine.

Chapter Five

Leisure Time and Hobbies

At the beginning of each chapter, I find myself wanting to declare how important the subject of the chapter is, and this one is no exception.

Your personal circumstances determine the time that is taken up with everyday living, and the time that is left to participate in leisure activities and hobbies.

The circumstances I refer to include the following:

- Do you work part time?

- How much of your time is spent volunteering?

- Are you a caregiver to an elderly person, sick person or child?

- Do your health concerns take up a lot of your time?

Your lives consist of things you must do and things you choose to do. If you divide your time into ten, the first seven life activities remain constant except in the amount of time spent on each. The last three, being optional, vary in length and participation. The options can change when you want change, when you want to enrich your life, and when you want the opportunity for experimentation and creativity. These last three are **me** oriented and you should not feel guilty about pursuing them. You must give yourself permission to enrich your life, to be creative and to do things that **you want** to do.

The concept of dividing time into ten would look like this:

1. Time for personal matters (examples: brushing teeth, housework)

2. Cooking and eating

3. Sleeping

4. Exercising, moving your body

5. Socializing and social obligations

6. Spiritual time including meditation and/ or prayer

7. Reading

8. Option #1

9. Option #2

10. Option #3

Unless you are restricted physically or mentally to only the most basic activities, I believe that you should make every attempt to include at least two or three options daily.

Choosing more than one option helps you keep a healthy perspective on your life. One example is this: If you are an avid reader and do nothing else, you may find yourself feeling confined by this narrow approach, and at some point you exhaust yourself and find that you have no alternative. However, if you set time aside each day for reading and then time for at least one other choice, you will always look forward to each with more anticipation and vigor. (I view reading as essential, but it could also be a choice.)

If and when you begin feeling that you have exhausted a hobby or leisure time activity, you must put it away for some time. The time to decide whether a new activity is called for or whether just a break is needed will vary. This time out may be a month, two months, six months or longer. While you are in a time out period, try something different. Take a course, or research and try something new on your own.

Some people do not seem to tire with their choices. You all know those who have had the same leisure time activity for years and still approach it with enthusiasm.

Some suggestions for the three optional activities are as follows:

1. *Use* your computer. You can word process (creatively), e-mail, use the Internet, and play games. Satisfying your curiosity, obtaining information and even locating new recipes are easy on the Internet.

2. *Play* board games that are not only fun but require a lot of mental acrobatics. You play these games with other people which make it a social activity as well. Some of my favorites are Pictionary, Trivial Pursuit, Balderdash and Master Mind.

3. *Play* bridge. This is a card game that you can take to many levels. You could become a social player and use it as a means for getting together with friends or meeting new people. You could also become very proficient and play in competitive situations where you could earn master

points. Either way, your brain will thank you every time you exercise it this way.

4. *Garden.* Grow a traditional vegetable garden or a clay pot garden. Take better care of an existing flower or rock garden, make changes or try new plants and care techniques. If you have not grown roses before, give them a try.

5. *Grow* houseplants. Succulents are fun to grow and they are good looking. Flowering plants can be a lot of work, but they do add a lot of color. Orchids may provide you with a challenge. The cacti family is great if you do not have regular small child visitors, and the vine family provides superior greenery. Experiment. My most recent challenge is growing hydrangeas indoors and out. Our climate may be too harsh for them in winter, and they need special protection. Indoors the leaves dry very easily. The challenge is in overcoming these problems.

6. *Participate* in sport or physical activity. While some sports give you more exercise than others, they are all worth doing if you get to socialize, move your body parts, learn and enjoy. The exercise component is addressed in the Chapter 4. Depending

again on your budget, conditioning level, health, time on hand and personal taste, here are some of the sports and activities you can choose from: golf, curling, cycling, swimming, a variety of handballs, basketball, volleyball, tennis, softball, slow-pitch, badminton, skating, hiking, walking, scuba diving, and bowling.

7. *Dance*. This particular activity can be learned at any age. Remember that not everyone will achieve the same level of proficiency. Do not allow the fear of failure to hold you back. Participating, learning, and enjoying the experience make dancing a worthwhile choice.

8. *Sing*. Join a choir or other singing group. This is a good example of an activity that can overlap with and fulfill other needs as well. Singing in church choir may fulfill part of your spiritual needs, and it is also a social activity.

9. *Become* involved in a musical or dramatic theatre group. You could act, sing, create costumes, build sets or be a front-of the-house volunteer.

10. *Coordinate* a readers' or library club if you enjoy organizing and record keeping.

You may want to do this for one or two reasons. Reading can be a social activity if you meet with others to discuss the books you have read. If you do not have access to a library, or one is just not located near you, organizing a book or library club may be an inexpensive way to read a lot of currently published books by exchanging them with others. Suppose that you have eight members in your club. Each would be responsible for buying one book that would be circulated among the members. Instead of purchasing eight books, you would only purchase one.

11. *Learn* to do something new. A book could be devoted to suggestions of things to try. Imagine. Ideas could range from learning to cook with a new ingredient, learning how to fly an airplane or learning how to e-mail.

12. *Try* a new art or craft. Your choice may be creative and fun to do. Ask for help from someone who has the skill, take a course or read and learn. Let your imagination fly. Your art or craft need not look like everyone else's.

I like to use what I learn in a course as a starting point, and then I experiment. Sometimes I am not creative enough to do that. Some things cannot be changed easily without losing essential technique. An example of this for me is papier tole. For that craft, I followed suggested techniques very carefully.

13. *Scrap book.* Become familiar with what it entails. This way of documenting your photos and memorabilia is not a one-time activity, but a long term commitment. It is time consuming, the supplies are costly, and they need to be replenished continually. Know that you will not be scrap booking all the time. You may require a substantial time commitment in the beginning, and later only when you have something new. To make five scrapbooks has become one of my goals and challenges. After five months of focused scrap booking, I completed only two thirds of the first scrap book before I needed a break.

14. *Cultivate* a new interest. Bird watching, fishing, or playing a musical instrument are only a few.

15. *Exercise* your mind daily with challenges such as SU DO KU puzzles, word jumbles and crossword puzzles.

Deciding what to do with your leisure or spare time should never be a chore. You need to approach it with determination, anticipation and a positive attitude.

Chapter Six

Travel and Vacationing

Travel is something that most of us want to experience. The word travel refers to two things: it can refer to the journey, or it can refer to the means you use to reach your destination.

The word vacation may conjure up a number of different images. Your own picture of a vacation will be shaped by your personal preferences, health, age and budget. These are some of the category possibilities:

1. *Visiting* with relatives or friends in their homes.

2. *Spending* time outdoors, camping, fishing, hiking or skiing or a combination of these activities.

3. *Leaving* your permanent home in favor of spending the colder months in a warmer

part of the world or vice versa. The Canadian snowbirds are noted for that. The term snowbirds refer to Canadians or Americans who spend several months in a warm location while it is cold in Canada and in the northern states.

4. *Working* in a different country, either intermittently or on a full-time basis over a period of time, such as a year or two.

5. *Traveling* short or long distances from home on day trips, week trips, seasonally or for years, in order to see as much as possible and learn new things.

6. *Cruising* has become a popular form of vacationing. New places can be visited while living in luxurious surroundings.

7. *Adventure-traveling* can include hiking in hiking-friendly countries, kayaking in unusual places, mountain climbing, going on an African safari and more. This may be the category least chosen by seniors since the choices are physically demanding.

Travel on a limited budget

Choosing from the variety of options is easier if you have a secure and substantial travel budget. However, if you want to travel and your finances are limited, there are ways to stretch your dollars.

For all the examples of travel options below, you need preparation time. You will require time to collect, time to research, and time to make arrangements.

1. *Register* with reward programs.

   - Collect air miles when you purchase the things you need, such as groceries, gas, appliances and other necessities. However, you need to be disciplined about not spending more than you can pay on your card at the end of the month.

   - Collect reward miles when you fly. These miles can be redeemed for flights, hotels, car rentals, and more. Air Canada's reward program is **Aeroplan.** To learn more about the program, go to www.aeroplan.com.

   - Contact other airlines for information about their reward programs.

2. *Join* a group that exchanges with hosts in other countries with the

understanding that you would be required to take your turn at being a host: www.friendshipforce.org.

Complete information in Chapter 15.

3. *Become* a house sitter for a homeowner in your own or a foreign country: www.housecarers.com.

4. *Become* a fractional owner of a condominium unit. If you are an owner and can exchange worldwide through one of the exchange agencies, your options are greatly enhanced. It is a very useful and usually comfortable way to see new places or vacation on the beaches of a warm climate.

5. *Rent* a condo, an apartment or a house. It is especially economical if you are vacationing with three to five other persons. You could rent by the week or month and share the costs while living in spacious well-furnished accommodations. Having meals in as often as you choose would help keep costs down.

6. **Take** a cruise.

   • *Investigate* becoming a working cruiser. In researching the possibility, I discovered that for a small fee of anywhere from $25.00 per day to one quarter the cost of one published fare, you and the person sharing your room may pay for the remainder of your cruise with a service that you would provide.

Some cruise lines make their own arrangements for guest crew. Each has slight variations or rules regarding guest crew. There are also agencies that recruit guest crew for some of the cruise lines. These positions are non-salaried positions. You could be a crafts instructor, lecturer, bridge director, or gentleman host and more. Depending on the cruise line, you may have the same privileges as full fare paying passengers. That includes staying in a stateroom and eating meals with the passengers. You may choose to leave the ship at ports of call (unless the service that you are providing is scheduled for that time). You may be asked not to participate in some activities where you would be taking prizes away from those paying full fare.

Guest crew may also be required to sleep in crew quarters and eat with the crew. You may not be comfortable with that scenario, and that may be your determinant about accepting or rejecting the position. Certain other restrictions may apply as well.

If you are interested, you can contact cruise lines by phone or e-mail and discover if a skill that you have can turn into a guest crew position for you. Try the **contact us** link on their websites or look for a phone number that you can use.

One agency that may be able to help is "Posh Talks": *www.poshtalks.com.*

They describe themselves as "The Premier Cruise Ship Assignment Agency".

- *Purchase* cruises tickets at reduced prices. You may be required to travel on short notice, cruise at the beginning or at the end of a season for that area, or book passage on repositioning cruises. Go to the websites of cruise lines and get some ideas. You can also book online, or you may prefer to talk to a travel agent or a cruise specialist. They may be familiar with information that you have not found in your search online. The place to start is to learn what constitutes a good deal, and then be prepared to wait for it.

7. *Exchange* your home with someone from your own country or a foreign country.

The other party would use your home and car for a specified period of time. At the very same time, you would use theirs. This option requires a lot of preparation, but as you can well imagine, the cost of your vacation would be considerably reduced. For more information go to this site: www.holi-swaps.com.

8. *Take* advantage of airline seat sales. You would be required to be vigilant. These sales are usually not advertised for a long period of time.

9. *Purchase* **flight passes**. This option is relatively new in air travel. Air Canada is a good example of an airline that offers these passes. You purchase four flight credits for your selected zone. It can be Western Canada, Eastern Canada, North America east or North America west. The cities in your zone are listed and you can choose when and where your credits are used. With careful planning, you can save using this method of travel. Similar plans are available in Australia and New Zealand, Europe and the USA.

10. *Purchase* **commuter passes**. These passes are restricted to designated zones; they vary in the number of credits you can

purchase, and they must be used in a specific time period.

One commuter pass, offered by Air Canada, is for Western Canada. Your choice is to purchase 10 or 20 flight credits. You will use one flight credit per direction (one flight) including connecting flights. An example is: Victoria to Edmonton via Vancouver and Calgary is considered one flight. In this example the credits are valid at five locations: Abbotsford, Calgary, Edmonton, Vancouver, and Victoria, and must be used within a one year period.

Purchasing a commuter pass should save you money. You can make comparisons with regularly posted fares before you commit.

For more information go online to www.aircanada.ca or call 1-888-247-2262.

Research the possibilities with the airline of your choice.

11. *Travel* by bus. GreyHound offers incentives for senior travel. Bus fares are cheaper on weekdays. Seniors, 62 years and older, can request a 10% discount. Two persons

traveling together may receive up to a 75% discount for the second person. With a Hosteling International membership card, you will be entitled to a 25% discount.

For more information go to www.greyhoundcanada.ca or dial 1-800-661-8747.

12. *Choose* your mode of travel wisely in order to save money. What are the pro and cons of each possibility?

Short distance travel

Let's first consider vacations within driving distance. Is your vehicle road worthy? How much will the repairs cost to prepare your vehicle for the trip? (Keep in mind that repairs in a place you are familiar with will likely be less expensive. The mechanic at home is probably someone you have used before and can trust.)

Long distance travel

For long distances, become familiar with your options. Investigate the cost for bus fares, train fares and airfares. Taking advantage of a seat sale may be your most viable option. For example, flying from Calgary to Toronto for $300.00 return fare would be a saving over driving. The drive would take about three or four days each way, during which time you would need motel rooms and many meals in addition to the cost of gas and related car expenses. Also consider whether you need a car at the destination. Would renting a car be less expensive when the whole picture is considered? Make your comparisons before you decide.

Train travel

Depending on the country of travel, the train may be your best choice. Look for specials and packages. If you are a Canadian planning to travel in Europe, using this option is recommended. There are substantial savings by buying your tickets in Canada before you go abroad.

When you buy Eurail tickets, you purchase tickets by the number of days that you want to use the ticket for the countries specified. You can travel an unlimited number of hours in one day.

On a recent trip, my husband and I had six day tickets valid in five countries. On one of those days, we boarded a train in Zurich, Switzerland, at 9:00 am. We arrived in Madrid, Spain, at 8:00 am the next morning. This was within a twenty-four hour period and therefore counted as one day of travel. The Eurail ticket savings are on longer trips.

If you use your day ticket between two cities that are near by, and that trip is your only travel for that

24 hour period, the cost for that day may not be economical. For short trips you may be wiser to use a bus.

If you are traveling long distances and you are unable to sleep on public transportation, then your decision may be an easy one. You would likely choose the quickest and most comfortable option.

Air travel

If you decide to fly, consider the following. Check with all available airlines. Compare weekdays versus week-end rates. Off season rates are less costly. Do you qualify for special discounts? Two examples are motor association member discounts or senior travelers' qualification for at least a 10% discount. The best way to book is to be flexible about both date and time of day. Early morning and late day rates may be less than daytime rates. Flying to airline hubs can be to your advantage or disadvantage. Some travel sites compare prices for airport choices in large centers. Researching the options is very important before booking.

If you are flexible, have plenty of time and are a competent Internet user, you can search for that information online as well as book online. When making a request, it is to your advantage to give a range of dates to determine the least expensive flights. Does the price quoted include taxes and fees?

After you have committed yourself, read your itinerary carefully. You may be flying to an alternative airport or departing from a secondary terminal. When my husband and I were leaving Madrid, we failed to notice our check-in terminal designation. The hotel shuttle delivered us to terminal A. When we realized that we were leaving from terminal B, we were stressed by the prospect of not getting there on time.

When buying your tickets online, a confirmation will be e-mailed to you. That confirmation should be printed and carried with you. Airlines may want to see it at check-in.

Some websites that may help you are listed in Chapter 15.

Whether you book through a travel agent or online, you should become familiar with the whole package before you commit to it. A discounted ticket becomes very expensive if you cannot use it.

Most airlines can be booked from their websites, and they have toll free phone numbers as well. Consolidators and discounters can also be found on the Internet. If you are going that route, you may want to charge your fares to a credit card that guarantees a refund if the tickets do not materialize. Does your credit card company provide that service? Is there a time restriction for a refund (usually seven days)? There are other reasons for using a credit card as your method of payment.

Refer to *HOW TO GET THE BEST DEAL EVERY TIME YOU TRAVEL*, page 21. Complete ordering information for this book is contained in #1, Chapter 15 of this book.

Travel deals that are advertised in pop-ups online or in any other unsolicited manner should be avoided.

The best time for calling airlines or visiting websites, is either late Friday when the deals are released or between midnight Tuesday and 1:00 A.M. on Wednesday when unsold tickets from Friday enter the system at a discount. Visit the sites several times to become familiar with their routines.

Many more options regarding air travel are discussed at length in:

HOW TO GET THE BEST DEAL EVERY TIME YOU TRAVEL.

For an abundance of international travel information, you can subscribe to a monthly publication called **International Travel News.**

For ordering information refer to #3, Chapter 15 of this book.

Preparing for your trip

Preparations need to be made if you are planning to leave your home for an extended period of time. These preparations fall into two categories. First you must prepare for the trip itself, and then you must prepare your home for your absence.

These to-do lists should help you be prepared for worry free travel.

Trip Preparation

1. *Buy* travel medical insurance. You may already have adequate coverage, but that should be reviewed, especially if you travel outside your own country. Medical costs incurred in other countries may be only partially covered by your plan at home or not at all.

   Price the coverage that you need with several insurance companies before you buy. Prices will be determined by the length of your stay, by pre-existing medical conditions, and by your age. You should inquire if you would be able to extend your coverage on short notice and how much that would cost you. Carry the company's claim number with you and the phone number you might need to extend your coverage.

Here is an example of the importance of carrying medical insurance: After being away from home for ten days, on a trip to Florida, I was in pain from an in-grown toe nail. I needed medical attention immediately. I called the claims department of our insurance provider, and after receiving a claim number, I proceeded to have medical attention at the nearest facility. When all was done, our insurance company paid about $700.00 U.S. for the services that I received. My husband and I were very pleased that we did not have to pay for this treatment out of our travel budget.

2. *Carry* important phone numbers with you.

   a). Family

   b). Credit cards' 800 numbers

   c). Insurance company claim number

   d). Phone numbers for Canadian consular offices in the countries you will be visiting

   e). Other numbers that are pertinent to you

3. *Carry* a copy of your "Personal Directive" and leave one with someone at home. (Details in chapter 10)

4. *Bring* film for your camera and adequate batteries, or a charger, and chips for your digital camera. If you choose not to bring all those supplies, plan exactly how you will deal with your camera needs. Supplies are usually less expensive at home, especially if you are traveling abroad. If the country that you are visiting operates on a different electrical voltage, you should bring the appropriate converter and transformer, not only for charging your digital camera batteries, but for your electrical razor, curling iron, blow dryer and iron.

Many hotels and condos now supply blow dryers. You may want to ask before you pack yours.

5. *Take* a supply of sunscreen with UV ray protection.

6. *Know* how to access money. Remember your Personal Identification Number (PIN) or numbers. Know if you can get cash advances on your credit cards and know the amount you can get. Some of your money should be in travelers' cheques. The records and the telephone

number for calling the issuer should be carried separate from the cheques. My husband and I have used American Express and recommend them. We had a card replaced very promptly when the machines were unable to read the old one. The company has offices in most foreign cites where you can obtain cash or get a replacement card.

A **tip** to travelers using debit or credit cards for the purpose of obtaining money.

Our tour guide in Spain informed us that if a machine swallows your card in order to process the transaction, the card should never be inserted more than twice. If you make an error the second time, go to a different machine. Some machines are programmed to keep your card on the third attempt.

7. *Bring* sufficient medications to last the duration of your trip. Carry a *photocopy of your prescriptions* for emergencies. Ask your doctor to write your prescriptions legibly in an international language if you are visiting a country where a different language is spoken. That would allow pharmacists or doctors access to the information. A copy of your prescriptions may also be required at a border crossing as proof of your need for the drugs that

you are carrying. The medications should be carried in their original containers. Air lines now have the same requirements if your medications are in your carry-on bag.

After you arrive at your destination, the break in your routine is easier to deal with if you set out a week of medications in a container referred to previously in Chapter 2.

Bring several over-the–counter medicines with you in their original containers when your destination is outside Canada or the USA: antiseptic cream for insect bites, insect repellent, motion sickness remedy, preparation to stop diarrhea, painkillers, and laxative.

Note: Health Canada recently approved **Dukoral,** which is a drinkable vaccine that guards against travellers' diarrhea caused by cholera and Eschericha coli. For more information go to: www.phac-aspc. gc.ca, or talk to your pharmacist.

8. *Update* your e-mail address book.

9. *Make* a comprehensive list of things that you want to take with you. I started doing this as a matter of survival. Being a person who packs at the very last minute, I tend to forget necessities. Having a list helps

me immensely. Where you are going and how long you are staying would dictate how many of the items you would use at any particular time. Make copies of your list so that you have one each time you need it. I am including one for women, one for men, a third for non-clothing items and a fourth for vacations that require you to bring cooking utensils and food. Examples are in APPENDIX C.

10. *Roll* your clothing when you pack. That seems to save space and eliminates the need for ironing as well.

11. *Select* clothing that is made from synthetic fabrics that do not crease easily. Mixing and matching items saves space, since you do not pack as much. I usually bring a microfibre sweater. I wear it when I need layers, or use it as a neck roll when on public transportation. It is useful for sleeping in when I have inadequate covers, and it washes easily in a sink.

12. *Leave* your diamond ring and other valuable jewelry at home.

13. *Pack* items such as toothpaste in re-sealable plastic bags.

14. *Bring* and *carry* small packs of tissues. The tissues can serve several purposes. In some countries you cannot count on the luxury of having toilet tissue in bathrooms.

15. *Save* space in your luggage by stuffing your shoes with small items like socks, undergarments, and jewelry.

16. *Pre-plan* your daily menus if you are camping, going on a driving stop-when-you-feel-like-it trip, or to your condo or cabin. Pre-planning meals will make your grocery list easier to plan.

17. *Call* the airline to learn if meals will be served during your flight. There have been changes to air travel in recent years. You can no longer count on being fed while in the air. Food will not likely be served if your flight is less than three hours in duration. You may only be served a small snack. On international flights, you will probably be served a meal. Inquire and be prepared with your own supply of food if you have special needs and cannot wait. When determining your food needs, consider the time it will take to check in before your flight and the time to disembark. A three hour flight may actually take up to six or seven hours.

18. *Notify* the airline in advance if you have a dietary restriction. Make your request no later than 24 hours before the flight.

19. *Limit* what you bring in your carry-on or purse. What you are permitted to have in your carry-on should be determined by making inquiries with the airline.

    On a recent flight, my husband's toothpaste and shampoo were confiscated by security. Both were in his carry-on, and would not have been taken from him if they had been in his checked luggage.

20. *Secure* your luggage. Be certain that your luggage will arrive intact by securing each piece with a strap that is made for that purpose. Several times we have witnessed luggage on an airport carousel with garments hanging out of it. If you use a colored strap, your luggage will be easier to spot as it makes its way down the ramp.

    It is equally important to have your bags labeled with your name and city of your residence. If an unlabelled piece of luggage gets lost, it may be sent to a warehouse and eventually discarded.

21. *Become* informed about specific countries when you travel internationally. This information can be obtained from **Government of Canada Consular Affairs.** How to locate this information is in Chapter 15 of this book (**Services for seniors and non-seniors** #1) or from your travel agent upon request. These information sheets will advise you about currency, emergency contacts, specific laws that you should be aware of and much, much more. In Canada, valuable travel information can also be obtained at the office of your local Member of Parliament.

The government of Canada has diplomatic and consular offices in 180 foreign countries. Make note of the Canadian consulate office phone numbers for the countries you will be visiting and carry them with you at all times during your vacation.

22. *Determine* your vaccination needs at least six months prior to departure. Your destination will dictate your need to have specific vaccinations such as Hepatitis A and B, or you may need to bring malaria tablets.

23. *Renew* your passport. Many countries now require that your passport be valid for six

months beyond the date of departure from the country. To re-enter your home country, you require a valid passport as well.

Home Preparations

1. *Make* an itinerary and leave a copy with someone that you trust. Include the phone numbers where you can be reached in an emergency.

2. *Cancel* your newspaper, or better still, have someone collect it on a daily basis so that the routine seems normal at your home. Interested parties such as home invaders may be watching for changes.

3. *Ask* someone to clean your walks and driveway after snowfalls.

4. *Arrange* to have your lawn mowed. An unattended lawn may attract unwanted attention.

5. *Have* an exterior light on a motion sensor, especially at the side or rear of your home. You could also leave a light on in the house and ask someone to rotate its location at least every second day.

6. *Notify* the police about your absence. They may drive by your property occasionally as they make their regular rounds.

7. *Feel* relaxed about leaving your home by finding someone to house sit. This person moves in and lives in your house. A university student is a good choice. A month or two of rent-free living in exchange for looking after your home can be a welcome arrangement for the student and result in a worry-free vacation for you. You would need to leave an extensive list of things to be looked after along with your routines, so that, once again, the home does not attract attention. Also leave a list of telephone numbers to call in emergencies. For the sake of speed and efficiency, leave the phone numbers for the police, fire emergency service and ambulance, and any other that you feel he or she may need.

Do not make the house sitter guess what is expected of him or her. Make a list that covers all expectations. Brief the sitter before you leave. Failing to leave a list in written form is asking for things to be forgotten. Even a person with a good memory may forget some important items.

Leaving a copy of your itinerary with the sitter would give him or her the opportunity to communicate if needed. The sitter should also have access to your insurance company claims number or that of a third party whom you are trusting to deal with emergencies.

8. Prepare for someone to check on your home at least every second or third day if you are unable to arrange for a house sitter. Check with your insurance company. Your policy most likely requires that someone look in on your home every so many days for your insurance to remain valid. Again, supply that person with a list of what to look for and the telephone numbers of whom to call if something goes wrong.

9. *Turn* your thermostat down to about 15 or 16 degrees C or 60 degrees F in cold climates if no one is living in your home.

10. *Double-check* that all doors are *locked*, and that the iron, curling iron, coffee pot, toaster and other small appliances are unplugged. Have you ever spent a day or two agonizing about the possibility that you left the iron on and needlessly spoiled your weekend? We have. Now we unplug the appliances habitually.

11. *Take* out the trash from all containers, and not just the ones with perishables. Someone may have dropped a banana peel or other perishable in a bin that is usually not used for that purpose.

12. *Turn* to OFF an old-style answering machine. All those beeps tell others that you have been away for some time.

13. *Leave* your home with the appearance of being lived in.

14. *Repair* items inside and outside your home and your yard. Prune branches away from windows. Attend to anything else that would invite intruders.

15. *Put* valuables that are easily carried away in a safe place. Your barbeque should be in your garage or shed out of sight.

16. *Hook* up a radio and a few lamps to timers.

17. *Leave* your lawn sprinklers hooked up to timers, just as if you were at home.

18. *Arrange* to have your mail held for you at the post office, or have someone collect it on a regular basis.

19. *Turn* water off in areas such as the laundry room. If you are a rural dweller, you may want to unplug your water pump.

20. *Pay* your monthly utility bills before you leave. If you plan to be away for a longer period, make arrangements for payment so that you are not in arrears when you return.

Whether you choose adventure, socializing, recreation or learning as your vehicle, getting away for the purpose of relaxation, fun, and new experiences is what a vacation is about. Choosing to be prepared may increase the ease with which you leave your home and help determine the success of your vacation.

Chapter Seven

We Are Social Creatures

All of us, as human beings, are the same in that we need social contact with other human beings. However, we do differ in the nature and in the quantity of social interaction that we desire.

The primary social contact that most of us have is with a spouse, partner or companion. From there we reach out to family, extended family, friends, co-workers, colleagues and acquaintances. In relationships with each of these groups, we fulfill our specific social needs of love, companionship, camaraderie, emotional support, and professional support.

The reality of many people's lives is that some or many of these social connections do not exist, or they choose not to reach out to the connections they have.

Another reality is that a smaller number of us overextend ourselves, and as a result we have difficulty creating bonds that could be achieved with a more concentrated effort.

To determine your social interaction level, each of you must first be familiar with your own comfort zone of social contact. That is your balance between personal time and social time. Is your personal/social balance 50/50, 20/80, 70/30, or some other ratio?

Is your present level of social interaction somewhere in your comfort zone, or do you need to become more involved or less involved?

If you need more social contact, what can *you* do to change that? The answer is **GO-CEP**. More specifically you can **give, organize, cultivate, extend,** and **participate**.

As I discuss each of these strategies, you will soon see that many overlap, and you may choose to place the overlapping ones in a different category.

Here are suggestions for the five strategies:

A. **GIVE**: Volunteer some of your time.

- Sit on a board of a service-providing agency.

- Be a member of a charitable committee.

- Volunteer at a hospital.

- Become a member of a service group or club such as hospital auxiliary or Meals on Wheels.

- Act as a host or hostess at a museum.

- Help family with baby-sitting occasionally; accompany grandchildren to games, concerts and performances.

- Inquire whether you could assist in some capacity with the fire department.

- Assist at your grandchildren's school as a room helper or a reader.

- Support your art gallery with the gift of time.

- Mentor or tutor a teenager.

- Read with a primary grade student at his/her school.

B. **ORGANIZE:** Take on a leadership role.

- Organize a neighborhood garage sale.

- Organize a reading group. Exchange books and use these books as a reason to get together and have discussions.

- Organize a group that would exchange videos or DVDs.

- Lead a group, or just participate in a letter-writing campaign for a political or social cause.

- Become active in environmental causes.

- Organize a league or event: senior's golf, fun curling bonspiel, bridge club, cribbage games, shuffleboard tournament, horseshoes, bowling, or a day cultural trip.

- Offer your home for a specific craft lesson or workshop.

- Give basic computer and Internet lessons to friends or neighbors.

C. **CULTIVATE**: Create bonds with family and friends.

1. Family relationships:

    - Have lunch (in or out) with one grandchild at a time. Make that one grandchild special for a day, and take each grandchild out in turn. If you have a number of grandchildren, once per year would suffice.

    - Spend more time with a grandchild who seems needy for the attention of others, especially that of an adult. You may be in a position to give the child a new perspective on matters.

    - Foster special relationships with other family members by doing things with or for them: Make an occasional meal for one that lives alone, sew something special for one, golf with another and so on.

2. Friendships:

    - Host a card or games night.

- Get a walking companion.

- Ask someone to travel with you.

- Invite someone you know for lunch or dinner, either at home or out. Remember to include friends who have, through divorce or death, lost a partner.

3. Cultural Group Membership:

- monthly movie

- stage performances

- book club

- bridge club

- pottery guild

- quilting group

- discussion group

D. **EXTEND:** Reach out to your community.

- Offer your services to a neighbor. For example, cut the lawn for someone who is less able than you.

- Offer to shovel the walks.

- Look after a neighbor's home when he/she is on vacation.

- Bring a meal to a sick friend or neighbor.

- Offer to run an errand for another while you are running one for yourself.

- Coach a team sport.

- Take turns driving to and from mutual activities.

- Make minor home repairs for someone who is not able or not skilled. You could exchange your service for something that the neighbor is proficient at doing.

- Offer to organize or run a club or activity for those with a mutual interest.

E. **PARTICIPATE**: Get involved in community events.

- A block party

- A neighborhood garage sale

- A sport or activity such as golf, horseshoes, bowling, curling

- A bridge group or club

- An exercise program that includes other people

- A community theater group

- Membership in the *RED HAT SOCIETY*: a sisterhood for senior women with no rules. The goal is to cultivate friendships and have good times: www.redhatsociety.com. There are many existing chapters throughout Canada and the USA.

As you were reading these suggestions, you probably thought of several others. Now get started! One at a time is best. If you realize that one choice turned out to be unwise, select another one.

In examining your own social involvement, you may surprise yourself. You may be more social than you realize, or you may conclude that you need to interact more. Only you can make that determination and act accordingly.

Chapter Eight

Living Alone

All the topics addressed in the book would apply to you whether you live alone or with another person. There are some exceptions for those who live alone.

There are two reasons why people live alone. The first one is because they choose to live alone. The second is a matter of circumstance. It could be as a result of a divorce, having a spouse or partner in a care facility or death.

1. Living alone as a result of death can be difficult. Grieving and getting on with your life is a challenge. The *Saying Farewell Handbook*, referred to in Chapter 12, describes grieving as "…a natural, human reaction to loss and is a part of the healing process."

This handbook suggests how to locate support groups and agencies that can assist you in your bereavement.

One of my friends named other challenges that arise as a result of losing a partner. A few of those challenges stood out:

- The experience of coming home to an empty house and knowing that you will remain alone can be unsettling.

- Disposing of the personal items of the deceased partner can be very difficult.

- Learning to live in a couples-oriented world, one that you are accustomed to and find yourself left out of, can be depressing and lonely.

2. Motivating yourself to make healthy meals takes determination. When I think back to a time when I lived alone, I recall that it was much easier to make a hotdog and call it a meal than to make a balanced meal. It seems that eating is a social activity, and sharing a meal with

someone else makes it more pleasant to prepare and eat.

3. Shopping for groceries, when you only have yourself to think of, can take more discipline. I sometimes indulged myself with foods that were quick to prepare but they were not necessarily nutritionally sound choices.

4. Considering housing options can be a challenge. Should you maintain a larger home, or should you choose an apartment, condo, smaller home, or possibly a mobile home? You may need to consider these factors:

   • Do you want to be bothered with home maintenance?

   • Do you want to grow a garden?

   • Are you willing to mow your lawn and shovel snow?

   • Is your budget flexible enough to hire help with the above?

5. Maintaining home security may be more of an issue if you live alone. To insure safety, obvious measures may be taken to make your home less accessible. Repairing

windows or doors, pruning shrubs that obstruct windows, mowing your lawn, and shoveling the snow, all give a home that lived-in and looked-after appearance. A place that looks neglected may be more enticing to intruders.

You can purchase added home security from a variety of companies who specialize in that area.

6. Traveling may be more difficult if you are alone, but not necessarily. There are many companies that specialize in group travel. A travel agent can arrange group travel for you, or you can use the Internet to arrange for your own adventures.

Accommodations would be more expensive if you buy single versus double. Your other costs should be the same.

Learn travel tips for singles, from a book called **Fly Solo: The 50 Best Places for a Girl to Travel Alone** by Teresa Rodrigues Williamson. This book will help you determine what destinations are suitable for a single traveler.

Traveling alone by motor vehicle may be a challenge. I have tried listening to books on tape while I drive and highly recommend it. You do not dwell on being alone and you are entertained. In this way the time passes more quickly.

When traveling alone, you need to be more vigilant with safety issues.

• Is your vehicle road worthy?

• Do you carry a cell phone?

• Do you know important numbers such as the police without having to stop and search for them?

• When you stop, are you aware of your surroundings?

• Do you stop in well lit places?

These are considerations when you are traveling with another person as well.

7. Motivating yourself to act may be accentuated if you are living alone.

I find that I need to make a conscious commitment in order to be motivated. Leaving something to chance decreases the likelihood of it happening. An example is my participation in the game of curling.

When I make a commitment by paying my dues and joining a team at the beginning of a season, I am motivated to act.

This lack of motivation may be more of a problem as you age.

8. Participating in social interaction may be the biggest challenge for those who live alone. In a conversation with another person, you may be required to problem solve, or make decisions or just enjoy the warmth of human contact. However, when you live alone, you likely watch more TV. This passive activity would not be as stimulating as interacting with others. Perhaps the choices of programming could compensate somewhat. Programs such as *Jeopardy* give an opportunity to think, problem solve and compete.

Solutions to satisfying the need to socialize and combat loneliness are likely numerous. Taking part in the activities of a senior citizens' center, enrolling in a course, or participating with others in a common interest are a few.

9. Having friends is important to us all, and to those who live alone, perhaps more so.

Friends are needed to share experiences, memories, sadness, joy and laughter.

You should keep in mind that dwelling on medical problems is an easy way to frighten friends away or shorten their visits.

10. Having a pet can assist in combating some of the loneliness. The decision to have a pet is a very personal one, since having a pet creates responsibilities that you may not anticipate.

11. Becoming more elderly and less able to move about freely seems to make living alone more of an issue. Your absence of social stimulation may be evident to others. Family, friends, neighbors and groups (fellow church members, for example) should be watchful and create situations where social contact continues. Their caring gestures may be as small as paying a short visit on a regular basis, phoning often to inquire about the person's well-being, asking if a ride is needed to an appointment, assisting with grocery shopping, inviting the person to lunch, or assisting with a chore.

If you talked to all the people that you know who live alone, you are likely to collect an equal number of additional challenges that they collectively face. What is your unique challenge as a person who lives alone, and how do you meet this challenge?

Chapter Nine

Setting Boundaries with Your Adult Children

Years ago parents and adult children had a very different relationship to what is true now. Parents did their best to educate their children about how to live and how to cherish the values that the parents held dear. It was understood that when the children, as young adults, left home, they were on their own. That meant that they were old enough to make good judgments in all adult decision making. Whether the choices made were wise or unwise, the adult children were expected to live with the consequences without asking the parents to bear those consequences with them.

This was the nature of the parent and young adult relationships of my generation.

Sometime between then and now that relationship changed. It seems that parents have become generally wealthier, and consequently the children have many more things. Many families go on regular vacations; children receive better educations; most families own homes; all needs are usually satisfied in most homes, and material wants are purchased for the adults and the children.

As these children become adults, their expectations are comparatively different. Once young adults expected to start with nothing and work their way slowly to home ownership and the ownership of other material needs and wants. Now they expect to acquire what they grew up with immediately upon leaving home.

Many of these young adults turn to the parents with financial and material demands, for psychological support, or with demands of time.

The parents, in most instances, are quite willing to share in one or all of the above. How much to share is the challenge. As difficult as this question is, it must be dealt with, and boundaries must be set.

Child care concerns

For some, perhaps the most difficult and yet most commonly-needed boundary to establish is how much and under what circumstances will you, the parent, be your grandchildren's caregiver. Today's families are usually very close in the emotional sense if not by proximity. Consequently setting that boundary can be a sensitive issue.

My observation is that a small number of adult children make demands on their parents with an *attitude of entitlement*. They expect the requests made of their parents will be met. Each family situation needs to be weighed independently to determine if the demands are reasonable.

Have you justified one of your decisions about an uncomfortable request or demand from your children with one of the following statements?

- "I *want* to be with my grandchildren."

- "If I don't help them, who will?"

- "I *am* family and family should help."

These reasons are all very noble and caring. But have you remembered to take *your* needs into account?

Have you also been heard to murmur one of the following?

- "I cannot do --------- because I have the grandchildren."

- "We'd like to go on a vacation, but who would look after the grandchildren?"

- "We do not have the money because we spent it on the children and grandchildren."

- "We feel like we are being used, but we do not want to voice our feelings for fear of negative consequences."

When sorting out your feelings and putting this relationship into perspective, ask yourself the following:

- "Is my child's reason for requesting my time a *need* or a *want?*"

- "Whose children are the grandchildren?"

- "Who should be responsible for the grandchildren?"

- "Are we, the parents, interfering by making ourselves so available? Would our children behave more maturely and responsibly toward their own nest if we were not as available?"

- "Are we contributing to our child's inability to care for her/his family?"

Understandings

The answer to this dilemma is not cut and dry, and it is not the same for everyone. Perhaps the answer lies in some form of compromise.

It might be helpful to start with some basic understandings:

- As dearly as you love your grandchildren, they are your *grandchildren*.

- Their parents (your children) are responsible for the grandchildren's well being and nurturing.

- If you allow your children to use you as convenient babysitters, your children may not be given the opportunity to develop into responsible independent adults.

- You have a life of your own, and if you don't should you be building one? **Hopefully your children and grandchildren are a very important part of your life. However, in most instances they should not be allowed to control it**.

- Although you would do everything in your power to be a caregiver to your grandchildren in circumstances of need, under most circumstances, your role as caregiver should be part-time.

Exceptions

1. The most obvious exception is one where your single daughter decides to keep her baby. The assumption is that the sperm donor does not support your daughter emotionally and does not behave as a loving father would to your grandchild.

   In this instance, the grandchild needs to be considered first. The grandchild should not be punished for the choices of his/her parents. Your duty as parents is to assist the daughter in establishing a life, as in getting an education. Your duty as grandparents is to be your grandchild's full-time care giver. Support your daughter emotionally by helping her set goals and formulate a plan for becoming an independent adult.

2. Perhaps the most common circumstance today, when your help may be required, is when your son or daughter is going through a divorce. Assistance may extend to temporary housing, childcare, and emotional support. Comforting arms and quiet unemotional words from you the caring grandparents may be very important

to your grandchildren's adjustment to their new reality. Your role can be to provide a place where the grandchildren feel secure both emotionally and physically.

3. Another exception is where your child's family is dysfunctional. This may be due to alcoholism or drug abuse by your child or his/her spouse. The grandchildren are powerless, and if you the grandparents are able to give their lives some normality, you would be giving them a precious gift.

4. Finally, your child and his/her spouse may be unable to be normal caregivers to your grandchildren. One parent may be hospitalized, handicapped, bedridden, or deceased. In these instances your grandchildren would need all the love and care that you can give. As grandparents you would provide physical and emotional care until such a time that the family is able to be the caregivers again.

Grandparents' considerations

- What is your physical and mental health?

- Are you remembering that you are helping out and not taking over? Adult children and their families need space from their parents and grandparents.

- Are your priorities, obligations and retirement dreams being respected by your children?

- Are you in a financial position to help?

Compromises

Finally, let's look at compromises. If adult children have asked you to play a role in the care-giving of your grandchildren, the time to set boundaries is now. Being honest about everyone's needs is essential.

- If the parents are both working, you could offer to be the caregiver when a grandchild is sick.

- You could be available for short periods of time when the parents want an adult-only vacation. The grandchildren's stay with you could be called a vacation.

- As a compromise to full-time care giving, offer a couple of days a week. That will still leave you with time for your own pursuits.

- You can pick a grandchild up after school and deliver him/her to an after-school activity. In this way you would have the opportunity to enjoy watching and cheering for your grandchild.

- Caring for the grandchildren on special occasions could be considered an exception to normal childcare arrangements.

- You could help out until other arrangements are made if regular childcare suddenly becomes unavailable.

This, in my view, is the touchiest subject in family relationships. We clearly have so many considerations to keep in mind. Making the right choice can be a difficult challenge.

Chapter Ten

Financial & Legal Matters

Plan for wealth accumulation

Financial planning for retirement is a subject that has been addressed by many authors. Most of us are concerned about how we will manage financially after we retire; consequently, it is the aspect of retirement that is planned for most often.

If you have not addressed your own plan for wealth accumulation, it is likely not too late to start. How much will you need in retirement, and what is your plan for getting there?

You must educate yourself! Take stock of what you already have.

Resources

Read about financial planning. Materials are available at a public library. There you can access books and a wide variety of newspapers. Another source is a bookstore with a computerized database. You will be able to search what is available on the subject of financial planning for retirement or general financial planning. Soon your ideas about what your personal plan should include will take shape.

Publications that are written specifically for seniors or for the retired audience often have a financial component. One such publication is *CARP-FOR THE FIFTY PLUS* (The Authoritative Magazine for Seasoned Canadians). The American version is the *AARP.*

The Internet is a source of information, especially if you want to verify or learn about the performance of a particular investment (mutual funds, stocks) or get particulars about a company.

When you are prepared to proceed with your plan, one of your options is to select a financial services representative to guide you. Ask friends and colleagues for recommendations and why they are pleased with the services they are receiving. It is important to get someone who is experienced and reputable. A company that meets my philosophy about financial planning for the future and provides a well rounded and common-sense approach is Primerica. They provide a comprehensive road map for their client's financial future. To learn more about the company, you can go to www.primerica.com. Phone numbers for Primerica representatives can be found in your local phone book.

It makes sense to start a financial savings program very early in your work life. However, if you have not done so, now is a good time to start. This option would be better than not addressing your retirement financial needs at all.

One thing that you cannot avoid in retirement is financial reality. You have accumulated a specific sum during your working life. Whether this sum is in real estate, stocks, mutual funds, a pension or other income, the choices you make in retirement are based on your personal financial reality. You must find a way to make the most with what you have.

Important Documents

You must plan for a time when you are not able to manage your own financial matters. There are also other decisions that should be made while you are able. These decisions will affect you when you are disabled or elderly. I am referring to a *will, a personal directive* and *an enduring power of attorney*. All adults, regardless of age, should have these prepared and stored in a place where they can be accessed by loved ones, executors or attorneys. If you are of retirement age and have not yet committed those decisions to paper, do not waste another minute. Have them written by you or for you now.

Will

Having a **will** at any age helps your family or estate acknowledge your wishes upon your death. If you die without a **will** (die intestate), the court would make the decisions for your loved ones.

If the expense of hiring a lawyer is your reason for not having a **will**, record your wishes in clear language, in either a handwritten or computer generated *will*. Give yourself plenty of time to write and rewrite so that you do not leave important matters out. When you are satisfied that the writing is completed, sign it in the presence of **two witnesses**. In Alberta, a hand written **will** does not require a witness. One that is mechanically printed requires two. Be sure that the witnesses also **sign, date** and **include their addresses.** You should then make a copy that would be kept in an accessible place. Tell your executor where it can be found. The original copy should be kept in your safety deposit box. Inform the executor where the box is located and where the key can be found.

If you can afford it, or if your wishes are complicated and you cannot give clear instructions on your own, have a lawyer write your wishes in a **will.**

Enduring Power of Attorney

Have an *Enduring Power of Attorney* **written, signed**, **witnessed** and **filed** in the same manner as the will.

In short, an *Enduring Power of Attorney* gives someone else, **named by you**, the legal authority to make decisions about your financial affairs in the event that you lose your mental capacity to do so. This could happen as a result of an automobile accident, stroke or because of general declining health in old age. You must state in your document when the authority comes into effect, whether immediately, or when you become mentally disabled.

This document can be written by you or by your lawyer. In Alberta, since December 1, 1997, a lawyer is not required to make one, but using one is advisable.

A *power of attorney* can also be given for limited powers. For example, if bills need to be paid while you are in a hospital, you can appoint someone to do that with a *power of attorney* for a specific bank. Authority is given by the *donor* (you) to an *attorney* (another person) to deal with your property.

Be sure to learn what the requirements are in your province or state.

Personal directive

Write a **personal directive.** This document allows you to appoint, while you are of sound mind, an **agent** who will make decisions about medical treatment and other personal matters in the event that you are unable to make these decisions for yourself. The other **personal matters** can be housing choices, non-financial legal matters, with whom you can associate, and end of life decisions. A comprehensive list can be obtained at: www.seniors.gov.ab.ca.

On the home page, click on **Office of the Public Guardian**. Then go to **Guardianship for Dependent Adults**, where you will find, **What a guardian is responsible for.** This site will help you decide what you want to include in your *personal directive*.

You should choose someone as your agent who will make decisions as you (the maker) would want them made. If you fail to have a *personal directive* when you become dependent, your court-appointed guardian may **not** be the person of your choice. A loved one may apply to become your guardian, but this process would take more time than if you had been proactive and written a *personal directive.*

You can choose to produce a handwritten or typed personal directive.

In Alberta, all *personal matters* can be covered if you write the following statement:

> "I appoint <u>name of agent or agents</u> to make all decisions on personal matters on my behalf."

Personal matters are considered to be anything of a non-financial nature that relate to you.

You can be specific about the *personal matters* if you wish. An example is cremation versus burial. What do you choose?

This declaration must be **signed by you, dated** and **witnessed by someone other than the appointed agent.**

Investigate what the requirements are in your own province or state.

In all three instances, having a **will,** an **enduring power of attorney,** and a **personal directive** would give you the choice of decision maker or makers as opposed to the court appointing the decision maker.

Listing your assets and liabilities

Make a list of your assets, liabilities and other important contacts that you update yearly. Keep your list with the three previous documents. There are many reasons for making this list. In the event of your death your family knows where your house is located, but what else will they need to know? Do they know the name of your insurance company? Do they know where your bank accounts are? Would your family know where to start?

This list is also for us. As we get older our memory gets shorter. When we deal with something on a regular basis, we are less likely to forget it. Suppose that you have a bank account that you have not used for some time. Are you likely to forget about it? Many have. Are you one of those who have forgotten?

Here are some suggestions for your list:

- Insurance company or companies' names and contact numbers

- Names of banks and account numbers

- Safety deposit box particulars

- Credit card information: names of companies and numbers

- Monthly payments, amounts and method of payments: computer, cheque, automatic bank payment and name of bank

- Membership to clubs such as book clubs

- Real estate holdings, addresses

- Investments such as stocks, bonds, mutual funds, annuities

- Pension particulars

- Reminders about pension plan/plans and Old Age Security options

- Location of deeds, leases

- Prepaid burial plans

- Location of birth certificate

Insurance

Examine your need and purchase insurance in these instances:

At the very least, you should carry a term insurance policy that is large enough to cover your liabilities, funeral and support for the person or persons who depend on your income. You would also want a separate policy for disability coverage if you are still a wage earner or if your income is dependent upon you having a healthy body. If you receive a pension or have investment income that would continue regardless of the state of your health, then you would need less or perhaps no coverage for disability.

Government programs

In Canada you **must apply** to receive *Canada Pension* and *Old Age Security*. You can apply for Canada Pension between the ages of 59 to 64 if you have contributed to the plan and are eligible. The amount of Canada Pension received is reduced proportionately, if you apply between the ages of 59 and 63. You lose a percentage yearly.

To receive Old Age Security benefits, you must wait to apply until you are 64, approximately six months prior to your 65th birthday. Most of us in Canada would be eligible for this benefit. You need to be familiar with some requirements.

To obtain application forms and more information you have these options:

> Phone: 1-800-277-9914 (for service in English)
>
> 1-800-277-9915 (for service in French)
>
> Online: www1.servicecanada.gc.ca
>
> Mail: For your regional office address, dial the toll free number or go online.

Be aware that you will be asked for your **social insurance number** regardless of how you choose to communicate.

What is the *Canada Pension Plan Survivor Benefit*? These are "…benefits that are paid to the deceased contributor's estate, surviving spouse or common-law partner and dependent children." There are three benefits and each has specific requirements. The first is a death benefit which is a one time lump-sum payment to a maximum of $2,500. The second is a survivor's pension, and the last is a children's benefit for dependent children. It is your responsibility to learn whether these apply to you.

Old Age Security recipients with a low income may also be eligible for another benefit from the *Income Security Program.*

You may be eligible for a *Guaranteed Income Supplement.* This program "...provides a monthly non-taxable benefit to low-income Old Age Security recipients living in Canada."

Receiving the *Guaranteed Income Supplement* is not automatic. You must qualify and apply to receive it.

In Alberta, low-income seniors may access programs and services by phoning 1-800-642-3853.

Locate the **Seniors' Information Line** for your jurisdiction and make inquiries.

It is easy to avoid dealing with matters that have been discussed in this chapter, yet you will likely agree that an examination of these personal items should be addressed sooner than later.

Chapter Eleven

Living with Illness

Most of us will be diagnosed with an illness or be informed of the illness of a loved one some time during our life time. It is difficult to predict how we would live with and manage these illnesses, since we all cope in our own ways.

In the late 1970's, my husband and I were both ill at the same time. Looking back at the experience now, it is revealing about what was foremost on our minds, and how some of our private thoughts differed from those that we shared with each other. Because the doctors were unable to diagnose my husband's illness, his health was fading and he was privately preparing for the worst. What he shared with us, his family, was optimism.

As a result of tests I had undergone, I had severe reactions that made me very ill. I was determined to get well so that I could resume my role as mother to our children and care giver to my husband.

Our daughter was eight years old and her behavior showed that she knew there was something very wrong. We tried to be reassuring and optimistic, but she sensed more and she reacted to what she was sensing. Our son, only five years of age, was the one who held our spirits from sinking with his hugs, smiles, positive comments and gestures.

Thankfully, in time, my husband was diagnosed and treated and I recovered. Looking back, it was interesting to learn how differently each of us dealt with illness in our family. The children likely dealt with our situation in an age-appropriate manner. Both my husband and I were instinctively looking out for the welfare of the other and the children, more than for our own well-being.

What does that tell us about how we deal with illness? To get a clearer picture, as well as another perspective, I asked some friends who have lived with illness in the past or are now in the present. What I learned from them was very informative. In our combined experience, we found that waiting for a diagnosis is very disturbing. While you wait, your imagination can be over-active. Your reaction to your conclusions could range from denial to fear in varying degrees.

We each have a personal level of awareness about what the possibilities are and that may impact our reaction to the diagnosis. Shock, surprise or anger may describe the initial reaction.

What follows the diagnosis is **living with the illness**. Each person, the one who is ill, the supporting partner, a family member or a friend, has his/her own way of dealing with this reality. Some of us, and possibly men more than women, are more private about how we cope. However, coping for all of us is a learning process.

The Canadian Cancer Society Website states that, "Everyone living with cancer deals with cancer in their own way." That is likely true for living with other diseases as well.

What happens to their partner impacts the spouse profoundly. Lifestyle, especially that of the partner with the illness, can dramatically change. If your body has undergone changes, your self image may also be affected.

A reassessment about what is important in our lives occurs. One friend explained that she saw the commercialism of Christmas in a new light. All the "window dressing" of Christmas seemed so unimportant when she was fighting a dreaded disease.

"Patience", according to another friend, "is needed on matters that the partner can do nothing about."

Seeking help

As I searched the numerous websites for helpful information, one thing became clear. There is a variety of support and information for families and persons in need. For those who do not use the Internet, a good place to start your search is with your health care professionals. Ask specific questions, and go back if you did not ask the right questions the first time. Some of your questions may be answered by phoning the seniors' information line. In Alberta the number is 1-800-642-3853.

The Canadian Cancer Society Website is a very comprehensive resource with regard to living with the illness. You can find it at www.canadiancancersociety.com Go from the **home page** to **Support Services** to **Coping with Cancer** to **Living with Cancer**.

The navigation bar on the left-hand side will lead you to these topics: **Managing stress, helping someone with cancer** and more.

The links on the right will lead you to such important issues as:

- **cancer and emotions**

- **tips for visiting**

- **ways to help**

- **keep offering support**

Ways to help link suggests practical supports that anyone can participate in.

Many of the ideas on this website would be useful regardless of the illness in question.

The same information can be accessed by dialing a toll free number (1-888-939-3333) to ask questions or request printed materials.

You may find it helpful to formulate your questions and even write them down in order to be assured that the information that you receive is the information that you want.

Other websites that you could go to are numerous. They each have their own point of view and their own choice of information. The **Heart and Stroke Foundation** offers great prevention information. The **American Diabetes Association** deals with prevention and how to live with diabetes.

To access the website of your choice, type in the name of the illness or the association, if you know its name, and follow the leads.

If it is the phone number or address that you require, your local *health unit* should be able to supply a pamphlet with that information and more.

If you are looking for information about one of the Rare Disorders, go to www.raredisorders.ca (CORD *or Canadian Organization for Rare Disorders*), and follow the links. Alternately, phone 1-877-302-7273 (toll free) or 416-969-7464 (long distance). This organization can also be reached by mail:

Canadian Organization for Rare Disorders
151 Bloor Street West, Suite 600
Toronto, Ontario, Canada M5S 1S4

The one thing that you can not predict is at what age you will be **living with illness.** It can happen anytime during your lifetime. It is safe to say that it is more likely to occur when you are in retirement or in your later years. You can consider yourself fortunate if you escape it altogether.

Is anyone ever prepared for what is to come? I am doubtful. The best you can do is have an attitude that you can and will know how to cope.

Chapter Twelve

Planning for the Final Years

You normally cannot predict when you will be in your final years. Because each person's time is unpredictable, the wise thing to do is to **plan early.**

You are preparing for two events. One is for the years when you will require some degree of care from others, and the second is your death.

In order for everything to happen as you would like, you must make your wishes known. If you spend your final years possessing a mind that is clear and able to make judgments, how lucky you would be. However, you must be prepared for the possibility that your mind may not be clear. Many diseases or conditions of the elderly cause psychological, physical, and mental impairment.

Being prepared

How do you prepare is the question.

Some of these preparations have been discussed in Chapter 10. Refer to that chapter for **wills, enduring power of attorney, personal directive,** and **listing of assets and liabilities**.

The following circumstances and preparations have not been discussed previously:

1. Be the kind of person who develops bonds with family, friends, and other acquaintances. Family members, who do not feel a connection to you, may not feel the need to visit you or assist you in your time of need.

2. Become aware of the levels of institutional care that are available. You and your family would then be able to seek the appropriate level when the need arises.

In Alberta there are several levels:

- Those who are able to care for themselves with minimal assistance may choose to remain in their home and access services.

- Your choice may be a lodge where you could remain relatively independent but could choose to participate in social activities with other residents.

- Assisted living is for those who need more help, such as with meals.

- The final level is nursing homes when a higher level of care is required.

3. Know the various help agencies and services that you may buy or access free of charge, if you are living independently in your home. I refer to **Home Care, Meals on Wheels, Lifeline,** the **fire department, ambulance, police, taxi** and **security services**.

   Lifeline is a program for those who still enjoy independent living but may require assistance as a result of a fall or medical emergency. The subscriber has 24 hours a day emergency help. Security is offered by means of a waterproof button worn around the neck or wrist. When the button is pushed, a radio signal is received at an emergency response center.

4. Downsize your home when it becomes too large to maintain. A condominium, townhouse, or senior apartment may be much more practical for you. Downsizing to a bungalow from a multi-level home may be a suitable intermediary step.

5. Recognize when it is time to dispose of some of your personal possessions. Keep the ones that still give you physical and emotional comfort. Dispose of the ones that you do not want or need. In my case, that could be up to one half of what I own.

   The possessions that you plan to leave to a specific loved one should be given while you can enjoy the giving.

6. Be realistic about the need to give up some or all of your driving privileges. I have witnessed seniors nearing ninety who refuse to admit that they are a hazard on the road. The family is then obligated to take measures that remove the driving privileges. This action insures not only the safety of the elderly driver, but of all others who are on the road.

   When you are in **early** retirement, you should decide that you will always consider safety first. I have not been driving long distances after dark for several years. My depth perception is poor, and I feel unsafe and tentative behind the wheel.

   Distance driving and night driving may be the two that you need to stop first, but others will follow. As your reaction time becomes slower, driving in cities and heavy traffic is hazardous. Failing eyesight, caused by conditions such as macular degeneration, makes driving unwise. When you have become an unsafe driver, it is time to stop driving voluntarily. Does this mean that you will be housebound? No, not if you choose not to be. Hiring a taxi, which is one option for transportation, costs less than owning and driving a vehicle.

7. Develop a network of people whom you may call upon for paid or unpaid assistance as you become less able to handle daily activities on your own. These may be family, extended family, friends, acquaintances or neighbors.

8. Arrange for the transfer or sale of business assets. Leaving this to family to struggle over after your departure may not be in their best interest. There are exceptions. If you have a family business and one or more will carry on with the running of the business, your only worry may be to ensure that the appropriate legal work is done. Be very specific in your *will* as well.

9. Leave specific instructions about the disposal of your home and personal items. If it is important to you that your clothes be donated to the Salvation Army, then make the organization known by name. You may wish to give a special book to a particular grandchild. Be specific about the name of the book and the name of the grandchild and maybe give a reason for your choice.

10. Discuss all decisions with family members to avoid surprises. Select your executor or executrix rationally. Ask for the person's permission to serve in that role and clearly state how he/she is to be remunerated. An article published in January, 2007, *Goodtimes*, a magazine for seniors, very succinctly discusses this subject and is well worth reading.

11. Cope with the loss of a loved one by death (bereavement) with assistance.

   A handbook titled **Saying Farewell** is available to read online or in printed form. It is "a helpful guide with information and forms to assist you through the death and dying process." You can request a copy by phoning 1-800-642-3853. You can also call 310-0000 (The Alberta Services

Call Center) or go to www.seniors.gov.
ab.ca. Click on **Information Services**
and then scroll down to **Saying Farewell**.
By clicking on the blue highlighted title,
you will access the entire handbook.

12. Discuss your wishes about your funeral,
memorial service or the absence of either
with your family. Prearrangements and
prepayment can be made with most
funeral companies if you so wish. If you
do not prepay for your funeral, you should
carry sufficient insurance or save money
dedicated for this purpose. You can also
pre-purchase a plot in a cemetery.

You do not want to think of your mortality, yet it
will happen regardless of your feelings about it. You
can and should be part of the decisions with regard
to your journey through your final years. In doing
so, you can make the transition easier for those that
you leave behind.

Chapter Thirteen

Hindsight

It has been almost six years since I wrote the first draft of this book. After my first grandchild was born, my focus changed. The manuscript was placed in my filing cabinet and has been resting there until recently.

In that time, several other things happened. I had to deal with illness in my family circle and friends. I was prepared for illness and death of the elderly people in my life, but not with the illness of those my age.

One of my goals was to volunteer within my community. As retirement approached, I committed myself to more than I could successfully handle. As time went on, I found that it was difficult to decide which I would discontinue. I should have been more realistic in the beginning and made my choices more wisely. I should have paid attention to advice my mother gave me in my youth, "Don't bite off more than you can chew!"

My scrap booking goal has not yet been met. Three more scrapbooks have been added since I started scrap booking, one for each grandchild. Realistically, my goals will have to be altered. I still plan to make a scrapbook for each person in my family, but in a shortened version.

I have learned several important things:

- To have an attitude of gratitude. I believe that we should be thankful for all things that are positive. Even on a bad day, we can always find something for which to be thankful.

After reading Art Linkletter's book, *Old Age is Not for Sissies*, I found his interpretation of attitude unforgettable:

> "It explains what makes us think and act like we're forty on our seventy-fifth birthday or what makes others think and behave as though they're seventy-five on their fortieth birthday."

What is your attitude?

- To distance myself from people who are poison in my life. I refer to negative controlling personalities. Distancing myself can be very difficult to do. It can, however, be an opportunity to establish a relationship with the same person on terms that give me more control.

- To see my doctor once a year, even if I think I am healthy.

- To discover that my grandchildren respond to my love for them with love, and that open arms are more important to them than an unwrinkled face.

- To know that good friends are gifts to be treasured.

- To realize that a challenge should be completed. The outcome may not be as I pictured it. Giving my best may be my reward.

The last seven years have taught me more than ever before to be flexible, to be inventive and to cherish the little things that bring meaning to my life.

Chapter Fourteen

Being Proactive (a summary)

Being prepared for the milestones in your life is not only wise but imperative. Can you imagine not preparing for a major vacation, a child's first day and year at school, your wedding, a move to a new job or a move to a new location far away from your family? Why should retirement be any different?

What is the very best that you can do? You can be proactive. You must do everything in your power to savor and protect your youth. You can look after your bodies by eating healthfully and exercising. You must make a habit of staying active and healthy spiritually, mentally, and psychologically. Lastly, you must also be prepared for the inevitability of old age and death.

Retirement is still all too often viewed as a time when you can do anything that you want to do, and that you will have plenty of time to plan when it happens. In my experience, there is some truth to that. However,

I have had more success with transition in areas that were pre-planned more extensively or at the very least were given thoughtful consideration.

Because many people now live into their 80's and often 90's, retirement years could span 1/3 or more of your life. That is certainly worth being prepared for.

Although being prepared is largely a state of mind, it has other components as well. You need a body that has been nurtured over time to sustain many more years of activity. You need psychological peace of mind and spiritual good health. All these need to be nurtured over the years preceding your retirement, as they are all interrelated and mutually supportive.

What you have to look forward to in retirement is a journey.

Do yourself a favor and plan *ahead* for what lies ahead.

Chapter Fifteen

Where to Find More Information (a partial list)

Travel

1. International Living:
   Webeditor@internationalliving.com
   Customer Service
   P.O. Box 968, Fredrick, MD 21705

   *HOW TO GET THE BEST DEAL
   EVERY TIME YOU TRAVEL*
   $22.95 US (includes shipping &
   handling)
   Best deals on airlines, hotels, car rentals
   and many helpful tips.

2. Elderhostel: www.elderhostel.org
   Dep't 14   PO Box 1751
   Wakefield, MA 01880-5751
   1-800-454-5768 (toll free)

The Website describes their service as follows: "…Elderhostel offers in-depth and behind the scenes learning experiences for almost every interest and ability… Enjoy these and many more with the not-for-profit leader in educational travel for older adults." They offer nearly 8000 programs a year in more than 90 countries.

3. *International Travel News: www. internationaltravelnews.com*
2628 El Camino Ave., Ste. A6
Sacramento, CA 95821-5925
Phone: 1-800-486-4968

Request a complimentary copy of this magazine by phone, by mail, or by e-mail: subscriptions@intltravelnews.com The magazine covers budget to luxury travel, and contains word-of-mouth travel information from people who have been there. The cost is $19.00 yearly U.S.

4. *Airline Consolidators Quick Reference:*
www.onthegopublishing.com
On The Go Publishing
P.O. Box 91033
Columbus, OH 43209

This paperback is available for download online at $21.95;   add $6.50 for shipping & handling if ordered by mail. The information online suggests this could be a valuable source. The book has pages on airlines information, hotels, currency evaluation, alternative travel, museums and more.

5. Bed and Breakfasts:

a). Educators' Bed and Breakfast:
www.educatortravel.com
Box 5279 Eugene, OR 97405
1-800-956-4822

Educators must join the network with a $36.00 yearly fee.

Stay with fellow educators for a $36.00 nightly fee per room. There is a $10.00 booking fee.

b). www.bedandbreakfastbyzip.com
c/o Maxim Technologies, LLC
3859 Chattahoochee Summit Dr.
Atlanta, GA   3039

Bed and Breakfasts listed are for all the states in the USA.

c). The Register Bed and Breakfast Directory:
www.travelassist.com
Follow the links to Canadian listings and links to other countries.

d). www.bbcanada.com
This is a listing of Bed & Breakfast locations in Canada.

6. Campus Lodging

Call individual university and college campuses to learn whether they offer lodging in the off season.

7. Arthur Frommer's Budget Travel:
www.frommers.com
link to: Bookingwhiz.com

This site contains a variety of travel deals that are updated every ten minutes: flights, hotels, car rentals, cruises, and holidays.
Please note that taxes and fees are additional.

8. Sky Auction: www.skyauction.com
Browse and make a bid on the flight of your choice.

9. Bestfares.com: www.bestfares.com
   This site offers European river cruises, all inclusive vacations, and **much more** can be found.

10. Holi-Swaps: www.holi-swaps.com
    9319 N 94th Way, Suite 500
    Scottsdale, AZ 85258
    Ph. 480-767-2753

    World-wide vacation homes are offered to exchange (swap, trade) or rent.

11. International Home Exchange Network: www.homexchange.com

12. HouseCarers.com: www.housecarers.com
    "Homeowners secure your home with a house sitter…
    Place a free confidential ad and we will forward responses for your consideration, from qualified candidates via our automated matching system."

13. Friendship Force International:
    www.friendshipforce.org
    Fax: 1-404-688-6148
    E-mail: ffi@friendshipforce.org
    34 Peachtree Street, Suite 900
    Atlanta, GA 30303 USA

Be a guest in someone's home. There are many locations around the world from which you can choose. Then take your turn at being a host.

14. Useful Travel Sites and Discounters:
www.lastminutetravel.com
www.bookingwiz.com
www.shermanstravel.com
www.orbitz.com
www.expedia.com
www.travelocity.com
www.cheaptickets.com

Note: We have used the site www. cheaptickets.com on several occasions. You can book flights and hotels or flights and car rentals at this site. Booking together, as a package, is usually less expensive.

Magazines for seniors

1. *GOOD TIMES*

The Canadian Magazine for Successful Retirement
25 Sheppard Ave. West Ste. 100
Toronto, ON   M2N 6S7
circulation@transcontinental.ca
$23.49 CDN, (price can vary by

province)
1-800-465-8443

2. CARP- FOR THE FIFTY PLUS
   (THE AUTHORATATIVE
   MAGAZINE FOR SEASONED
   CANADIANS)
   Kemur Publishing Co. Ltd.
   27 Queen St. E., Ste 702
   Toronto, ON M5C 2M6
   1-800-363-9736
   (in Toronto 416-363-8748)
   e-mail: carp@50Plus.com

   This organization publishes a member's
   directory to senior benefits, is active
   in advocacy for seniors, and promotes
   communications.

3. Professional organizations have
   magazines that target their retired
   members.
   An example is **ARTA News and Views
   (Alberta Retired Teachers'
   Association).**

Health and nutrition information

1. Service Canada: www.gc.ca
   Choose language→Services→Health

Then make your selection from the choices provided.

2. www.seniors.gov.ab.ca
This site contains useful information for seniors and others. For an overview of what you can find on the site, go to **Site Map**. Some useful links are **Publications and Forms** and **Related Links.** In related links, you can go to **Federal Programs, links to other provinces** and **Seniors' Associations and Clubs,** including Meals on Wheels. Information phone line: 1-800-642-3853

3. *www.healthfinder.gov/*
Government-sponsored gateway to online health information

4. www.*ama-assn.org/*
This is the official site of the American Medical Association and its journals.

5. *Prevention: www.prevention.com*
SMART WAYS TO LIVE WELL
Prevention Customer Service
P.O. Box 7319
Red Oak, IA 51591-0319
1-800-813-8070

6. *Alive*
   Canadian Journal of Health and
   Nutrition
   (Distributed through many Canadian
   Health Food Stores)
   Personal subscriptions 604-435-1919
   ext. 301

7. *Eat to Beat Low Blood Sugar*
   The Nutritional Plan to Overcome
   Hypoglycaemia
   By Martin Budd, N.D., D.O. and
   Maggie Budd

8. *The Healing Foods*
   The Ultimate Authority on the Curative
   Power of Nutrition
   By Patricia Hausman & Judith Benn
   Hurley

Services for seniors and non-seniors

1. Travel information: www.gc.ca
   Choose the language, and then click on
   Canada International on the left side
   navigation bar. Next go to **Services
   for Canadian Travellers.** You will
   find yourself on the **Consular Affairs**
   information page. On that page, go to
   the links that are important to you.

2. 2007 SENIORS' GUIDE TO FEDERAL PROGRAMS AND SERVICES:
   www.hc-sc.gc.ca/seniors-aines
   Print copies of publications can be ordered by contacting:
   Division of Aging and Seniors
   Public Health Agency of Canada
   Address Locator 1908A1
   200 Eglantine Driveway
   Ottawa, ON   K1A 0K9
   Telephone: (613) 952-7606
   Fax: (613) 957-7627
   E-mail: *SeniorsPubs@phac-aspc.gc.ca*

3. Service Canada: www.gc.ca
   This website is described as a "One-Stop Access" to programs and services for Canadians. Choose your language first. Then click on the **Service Canada** link on the left. Next go to the left side link **A to Z Services Index,** where you can search for the service of your choice by name, keyword, or department.
   For general inquiries you can also call 1-800-622-6232, or you may write to **Service Canada**, Ottawa, ON, K1A 0J9 Canada: Attn: Canada Inquiry Centre

4. *Canada, a society for all ages*
   1999 Community Kit for the

International Year of the Older Person
(Contains a list of national, provincial
and territorial senior organizations)
Source: public libraries

Magazines that may interest seniors and non-seniors

1. *CANADIAN GEOGRAPHIC*

2. *NATIONAL GEOGRAPHIC*

3. *EQUINOX,* Canada's Magazine of Discovery

4. *THE BEAVER* (Canadian History Journal)

5. *CANADIAN GARDENING*

6. *INTERNATIONAL WILDLIFE*

7. *SMITHSONIAN* (Science, biography, history)

8. *HARROWSMITH* (about country living)

APPENDIX A...RECIPES

In the recipes that follow, the left hand column shows the original ingredients, and the right hand shows the changes that have been made to improve the recipes nutritionally.

MEAT LOAF

1 lb. ground beef.....................	1 lb. lean ground beef
2 eggs	3 egg whites
½ cup dried bread crumbs	½ cup dried whole-wheat bread crumbs
½ cup diced celery	
¼ cup diced onions	
¼ cup milk	¼ cup skim milk
½ tsp. thyme or poultry seasoning	
½ tsp. salt	¼ tsp salt
dash of pepper	
tomato sauce 7.5 fl. oz. tin	
mozzarella cheese	skim milk mozzarella cheese
	or soy cheese

Mix first eight ingredients and bake in a loaf pan at 400 degrees F for about forty-five minutes. Spread the tomato sauce on top and then a layer of cheese before returning to the oven for about another fifteen to twenty minutes, or until the cheese has melted and lightly browned.

SCRAMBLED EGGS

5 eggs	8 egg whites and 3 yolks
1 tbsp. oil	1 tbsp. olive oil
5 strips of bacon	2 strips of bacon for taste
1 tbsp. scallions	
pepper to taste	
salt to taste	(do not add salt or cut amount by ½)

ADD:

1/8 cup green pepper, sliced

very thinly

¼ cup mushrooms, chopped

¼ of a tomato, seeded & cut into

small pieces

1 scant tsp. dried basil

First cut bacon into small pieces and fry to crisp but not dry. Use a paper towel to soak up the excess fat. Wipe the frying pan clean of grease. In olive oil, lightly sauté mushrooms and scallions. Add the eggs, salt and pepper. When the eggs are about three quarters done, add the green peppers, tomatoes, bacon and basil. Stir. Cook to the desired doneness.

LIMA BEANS WITH SOUR CREAM

1 lb. dried lima beans …………..
1 tsp. salt …………………………
½ cup chopped onions ………….
¼ lb. sliced fresh mushrooms …..
½ cup chopped green pepper …..
3 tbsp. butter or margarine………   3 tbsp. olive or canola oil
2 tbsp. flour ……………………..
2 tbsp. paprika…………………...
1 cup sour cream ………………..   1 cup fat-free sour cream
chopped parsley ………………..

Cover beans in cold water and soak overnight. The next day pour into a heavy saucepan, add enough water to cover beans, add salt and bring to a boil. Cover and simmer for about 1 ½ hours or until beans are tender. Drain and save the liquid. Sauté the onions, mushrooms and green pepper. Stir in the flour, paprika and 1 cup of the bean liquid. Cook and stir until thickened. Now stir in sour cream and beans. Heat thoroughly without boiling. Sprinkle with parsley.

This recipe can be halved.

MIRIAM'S BANANA LOAF

1 cup white sugar	1 cup brown sugar
½ cup butter or margarine	¼ cup olive oil and ¼ cup applesauce
2 eggs	3 egg whites and 1 yolk
3 tbsp. sour milk	
3 medium bananas (ripe)	
½ tsp. salt	(do not add salt or cut amount by ½)
½ tsp. baking soda	
2 cups white flour..............2 cups whole-wheat flour	
1 cup chopped walnuts	

Cream the sugar, olive oil and applesauce. Stir in beaten eggs, sour milk and mashed
bananas. Add baking soda and flour. Blend but do not beat. Fold the walnuts into the
mixture. Pour into a loaf pan that has been sprayed with light oil. Bake at 350 degrees F for
1 hour or until a toothpick inserted in the center comes out clean.

LAYERED SALAD

1 head iceberg lettuce, broken into
bite size pieces ....

bunch of fresh spinach, cut into

bite size pieces ....

1 10 oz. pkg. of frozen uncooked peas

1 bunch green onions, sliced ....
1 lb. crisp bacon, crumbled ....   **½ lb. bacon or less**
8 hard boiled eggs ....   **8 egg whites and 4 yolks**
1 ½ cups mayonnaise ....   **1 cup reduced fat mayonnaise and**
                                          ½ cup plain yogurt

                                          Add paprika to taste

In a 9 x13 inch glass baking dish, layer lettuce, spinach, peas, onions, sliced egg whites, crumbled egg yolks, and ½ the bacon. Seal with the mayonnaise and yogurt mixture. Refrigerate for 12-24 hours. Sprinkle with the remaining bacon and paprika before serving.

POTATO AND LEEK SOUP

1 ½ cups leeks, chopped (use white
and light green parts only) ....

½ cup onions chopped ....

1 clove garlic, minced .... **3 cloves garlic**

¼ cup margarine ....**1 tbsp. butter (for taste)**
plus 2 tbsp. olive oil

4 cups chicken broth .... **4 cups sodium-reduced**
chicken broth

2 cups raw potato, peeled and diced

1 cup whipping cream .... **1 cup half and half or ½**
cup whipping cream
plus ½ cup skim milk

1 tsp. salt ....
¼ tsp. pepper ....
green onions, finely chopped ....
(as much as you like)

Sauté leeks, onions and garlic in the butter and olive oil mixture. Add broth and potatoes
and cook. Puree mixture. Add cream, salt, and pepper. Before serving, heat without boiling
and garnish with the green onions.

TUNA CASSEROLE

1 pkg. (397g) chow mein noodles ...	8 oz. no yolk whole-wheat noodles
1 can (12 oz.) water- packed white tuna	
1 can mushroom soup	1 can sodium-reduced mushroom soup
1 cup milk	1 cup skim milk
1 cup celery, chopped	
½ cup green onions, chopped, white & light green parts only	

Add
½ pkg. (8oz.) broccoli florets
¼ cup shredded Parmesan
cheese (optional)

Whisk the mushroom soup and milk until smooth. Mix all other ingredients except cheese in a large bowl, and then stir in the soup mixture. Spread evenly in a 9 x 13inch baking dish. Sprinkle with the Parmesan cheese and bake for 50 minutes in a 350 degrees F oven.

OATMEAL PORRIDGE

This recipe is for one person.

½ cup quick-cooking rolled oats	½ cup large flake rolled oats
1 ½ cups boiling water	may need more
salt	just a pinch or none at all
milk	skim milk
sugar	½ tbsp. maple syrup or
	honey
	Add
	1 cup fresh fruit

If you are using quick-cooking rolled oats, 3 minutes at a slow boil is plenty of time. For the large flake, you will need more water and 10 - 15 minutes for cooking time.

Before eating the rolled oats, stir in your sweetener. In that way you will not taste pockets of sweetness. Use fruit that is ripe and sweet. You may be able to eat the rolled oats without any sweetener at all.

PAN FRIED WHITE FISH

2 fillets of your favorite fish ....

(I like cod or snapper.)

prepared batter	1/8 cup flour
3 tbsp. butter or margarine	1 tbsp. butter and 2 tbsp. olive or canola oil
½ tsp. garlic salt	¼ tsp. garlic salt and ¼ tsp. garlic powder

pepper to taste

In a small brown paper bag, place your flour, garlic salt, garlic powder and pepper. Shake to mix thoroughly. Add the fillets and shake to coat completely. Heat the skillet to a medium heat. Add 2 tbsp. of the butter and olive oil mixture. Fry the fish for about three minutes on the first side. After you turn the fish, add 1 more tbsp. of the butter and olive oil mixture if needed. The second side may need less time depending on the thickness of your fillet and your heat.

POTATO AND BEAN SALAD

1 lb. new red potatoes ....

1 lb. new small white potatoes .....

½ lb. fresh green beans ....

½ lb. fresh yellow beans ....

2 stalks celery, chopped ....

1 red pepper, chopped ....

1/3 cup fresh dill weed, chopped ...

1 cup mayonnaise salad dressing ...   ½ cup low fat mayonnaise salad
dressing
plus ½ cup plain yogurt

2 tsp. Dijon mustard ....

Pepper, freshly ground, to taste ...

Salt, to taste ....   Reduce the amount that you
usually use.

Half and cook unpeeled potatoes until tender. Cut beans into 2 inch (5 centimeter) lengths and blanche. (Add salt to the blanching liquid as that will allow the beans to retain their superb green color.) Immerse potatoes and beans in a cold water bath to stop the cooking process. When drained dry, combine all the ingredients and chill.

STRAWBERRY SHAKE

1 cup ice cream	1 cup plain yogurt
1 cup frozen strawberries	
2 tbsp. brown sugar, packed	1 tbsp. honey

Put all ingredients in a blender. Process until smooth.
Other fruits such as peaches or mangoes can be substituted.

LASAGNE

Use your favorite recipe .... Substitute the noodles
with whole-wheat noodles.
(They appear much whiter
after they have been cooked.)
Use low fat cheeses.
Drain the ground beef after you
brown it.

CORNED BEEF HERO SANDWICH

French bread	French bread style whole-wheat bread
2 tbsp. sour cream	2 tbsp. fat-free sour cream
1 tbsp. mayonnaise	1 tbsp. reduced-fat mayonnaise
1 tsp. chopped chives	or scallions
1 tsp. parsley flakes	or 2 tsp. fresh parsley
tomato slices	
corned beef slices	shaved, used sparingly
cheese slices	thin slices, used sparingly

Cut the bread horizontally and toast under a broiler. Butter each half sparingly. Mix sour cream, mayonnaise, chives and parsley. Spread on side that has a flat bottom. Layer with tomatoes, corned beef and cheese. Broil to melt and slightly brown the cheese. Cover with the other half of bread.

100% WHOLE-WHEAT BREAD (BREADMAKER)

1¼ cups water ....

2 tbsp. powdered milk ....

2 tbsp. shortening ....   2 tbsp. olive oil

1 tbsp. honey ....

1 tbsp. molasses ....   Omit and add another tbsp. of
                                     honey.

1 tsp. salt ....   Salt should not be reduced or
                                     eliminated in bread.

3 ¼ cups whole-wheat flour .....

1 ¼ tsp. yeast ....

ADD

When the kneading of the dough is
nearly completed, the signal for
 time to make additions
will sound. Add ½ cup mixture of
flax seeds, wheat germ, sesame
seeds and caraway seeds.

Follow the instructions for your bread maker. They will most likely ask you to measure and add the ingredients in the order given. Then follow the setting instructions for your machine to knead and bake the bread. The addition of the seeds will make the bread heavier.

You can set your bread machine on dough. When the dough has been kneaded and has risen, you can then shape it for the pan of your choice. Allow it to proof or rise again, and then bake it in your oven at 350 degrees F for about forty five to fifty minutes or 375 degrees F for about forty minutes.

THREE BEAN CASSEROLE

½ lb. ground beef	½ lb. lean ground beef
½ lb. bacon	¼ lb. meaty bacon
1 cup onion, chopped	1 ½ cups onion
1 clove garlic, minced	5 cloves garlic, minced
½ cup ketchup	
1 tbsp. salt	1 tsp. salt or less (Ketchup and beans are salted.)
¼ cup brown sugar	2 tbsp. honey or maple syrup
1 tbsp. dry mustard	
2 tbsp. vinegar	
1 can of lima beans (16oz.), drained	1 can lima beans (16 oz.) or cooked beans from dried. (Salt to taste.)
2 cans kidney beans (16 oz.), drained	1 can kidney beans (16 oz.) or cooked beans from dried (Salt to taste.)
3 cans baked beans in sauce (16 oz.).....................	1 can navy beans (16 oz.) or beans cooked from dried (salt to taste). Add ¼ cup ketchup and 1 tbsp. honey or maple syrup as well. You can add a cup or more of stock (chicken, vegetable, or beef) if the mixture is too dry for your liking.

Brown the ground beef, bacon, onion and garlic separately. Mix and combine with the remaining ingredients and bake covered at 350 degrees F for 45 minutes. If baked in a shallow baking dish, the baking time can be reduced. If baked in a deep dish, you may add 5-10 minutes.

This is a fairly large recipe, and the leftovers can be frozen for up to a month.

APPLE SAUCE

Apples (a red or yellow variety that
is ripe, but not over ripe)

1/4 cup sugar for each 6-8 apples …..   Eliminate the sugar.

If you would like some sweetness, you could add 1
tbsp. honey.

Add a combination of rind from
one orange, cinnamon or fresh
ginger, or all of the above.
You could start with ½ tsp.
cinnamon or ginger and then
adjust the amount to taste.

Peel and core the apples. Add the other ingredients. Cook until they are soft, but not
overcooked. Mash with a potato masher, and enjoy as a spread or on its own. If you like
apples, you will enjoy this recipe.

APPENDIX B ...MORE RECIPES

The recipes in Appendix B have been selected to reflect ingredients that are recommended for a healthy diet. They are also full of tasty flavors.

GRANOLA MIX

Source: *Unknown*

6 cups rolled oats

1 cup wheat germ

½ cup shelled sunflower seeds

½ cup sesame seeds

½ cup shredded coconut

½ cup chopped almonds

½ cup peanuts

1/3 cup vegetable oil

1/2 cup honey

1-2 cups raisins

In a large bowl combine the first 7 ingredients. In a saucepan, heat together oil and honey until warmed. Pour over the mixture in the large bowl and stir until evenly mixed. Spread the mixture evenly on two large baking pans. Bake in a 275 degrees F oven for about 30 minutes or until evenly browned. Stir 3 or 4 times during the last 15 minutes. Stir the raisins in during the last 10 minutes. Cool completely and store in a tightly covered container.

SALMON PATTIES

Source: *Prevention,* February 1999

2 cups flaked cooked salmon
1 egg or ¼ cup fat-free egg substitute
4 slices whole-wheat or oatmeal bread, crumbled
2 tbsp. low-fat or fat-free mayonnaise
2 tbsp. minced onion

In a bowl, gently mix salmon, egg, breadcrumbs, mayonnaise, and onions. Form into 4 patties.

Coat a nonstick skillet with cooking spray and place over med-high heat until hot. Add patties and cook 3 minutes before turning. Cook 3-5 minutes more, or until patties are firm and golden brown.

SMOOTHIE

Source: *Unknown*

In a high-speed blender make this nutritious, refreshing drink.

1 banana
6 large frozen strawberries or the equivalent in smaller sizes
4 tbsp. plain yogurt
1 cup skim milk
several ice cubes

Blend together for about 20 to 30 seconds. Pour into a large glass and enjoy.

SOUTHWESTERN PORK & BEAN SALAD

Source: *Cooking With Canola,* Canola Council of Canada

1 can (14 oz.) red kidney beans, rinsed and drained
1 can (7 oz.) corn kernels, drained
1 small carrot, chopped
½ red pepper, chopped
½ cup celery, sliced
2 green onions, chopped
1 tsp. dried parsley
1 cup cooked pork, cubed

Dressing:
¼ cup red wine vinegar
1 tbsp. canola oil
1 clove garlic, minced
¼ tsp. salt
pinch of freshly ground pepper
dash of hot pepper sauce

In a serving bowl gently toss salad ingredients together. Whisk dressing ingredients in a separate bowl. Pour over salad and toss gently. Chill for a minimum of 1 hour, stirring lightly a couple of times.

Variations: Eliminate the salt and the pork. Increase the garlic to 3 cloves, and substitute the oil used with olive oil. More parsley can be added.

Note: This salad is better the next day and will remain fresh for several days if refrigerated.

BACK PACKING MUFFINS

Source: *That's Trump*: Best of Bridge

3 cups flour
3 cups rolled oats
4 tsp. baking powder
1 ½ tsp. salt
1 tsp. nutmeg
1 tsp. cinnamon
¾ cup brown sugar
¾ cup white sugar
1 ½ cups margarine
1 cup flaked almonds
1 ½ cups chopped dates
1 ½ cups chopped dried apricots
rind of 1 orange

In an extra-large bowl or roasting pan, mix together first 7 ingredients. Cut in margarine using a pastry blender. Add next 4 ingredients. Measure into three equal batches and store in the refrigerator up to 4 weeks.

Variations: Use whole-wheat flour, ½ the suggested salt, non-hydrogenated margarine, and 1 ½ cups brown sugar only.

For one batch
1 ¼ cups buttermilk
1 egg, beaten
When ready to make muffins, add the buttermilk and egg to one batch of muffin mixture. Spoon into paper-lined muffin tins. Bake at 350 degrees F for 20 minutes.

BALSAMIC VINAIGRETTE

SOURCE: That's Trump: Best of Bridge

1/3 cup balsamic vinegar
¼ cup olive oil
¼ cup dry white wine
juice of 1 lime
salt and freshly ground pepper to taste
Variation: Add a tbsp. of Dijon mustard, smooth or grainy.

Pour vinegar (and mustard) into a small bowl and gradually whisk in oil. Then whisk in lime juice, season and store in the refrigerator. Just before serving, shake well and drizzle over greens.

CHICKPEA HUMMUS

Source: *Unknown*

1 can of chickpeas, (19 fl oz.) drained and rinsed

3 large garlic cloves

3 tbsp. lemon juice

¼ cup sesame tahini (sesame seed paste available in jars)

1/3 cup plain yogurt

½ tsp. ground cumin

¼ tsp. black pepper

Combine all the ingredients in the bowl of a food processor and process until smooth.

Note: I have used the hummus as a sandwich spread, as an hors d'oeuvre on toasted small garlic breads or as a dip for vegetables.

BUCKWHEAT CASSEROLE

Source: *Unknown*

The original recipe has been changed to reflect ingredients that I like and should have in my diet.

2 cups buckwheat groats
1 tin low sodium mushroom soup
4 cups water
1 clove garlic, minced
1 medium onion, chopped
2 tbsp. olive oil
1 tbsp. meaty bacon bits (can be real or ones made from soy)
½ cup mushrooms, chopped
freshly ground pepper

Sauté onions and garlic in olive oil. Wash buckwheat groats and pour along with onion and garlic into a 2 ½ L casserole dish. Add bacon bits and pepper. In another bowl whisk together water and mushroom soup. Pour over other ingredients in casserole dish and stir. Bake in a 425 degrees F oven for fifty minutes.

Note: This dish can be eaten alone as a meal, with a salad, or in place of potatoes, rice or pasta.

PROTEIN BURGERS

SOURCE: Beans & Rice: Company's Coming

¼ cup boiling water
¼ cup bulgar
3 tbsp. red lentils (boiling water to cover)
1 ¾ cups cooked dried navy beans
1 ½ tbsp. butter or hard margarine
1 ¼ cups onions, chopped
1 tsp. dried sweet basil
¾ tsp. salt
1/8 tsp. pepper
¼ tsp. garlic powder
1tbsp. gravy browner
hamburger buns

Pour first amount of boiling water over bulgur in a small bowl. Cover and let stand for 15 minutes.
Cook lentils until tender. Drain.
Add beans to lentils. Mash with bottom of a drinking glass. Heat oil in a frying pan. Sauté onion until soft. Turn into a separate bowl. Add remaining ingredients to onion and mix. Add bulgur and lentil mixtures. Mix well. Shape into patties using ¼ cup for each. Brown both sides in a frying pan using as little oil as you can. Serve as you would a burger with the trimmings you enjoy.

Variation: For this recipe I would add the suggested amount of salt. Serve on whole-wheat hamburger buns. The butter or margarine can be replaced with olive or canola oil.

MULTIGRAIN PUMPKIN SEED BREAD

Source: *Unknown*

4 eggs
1 cup granulated sugar
11/4 cups dark brown sugar
1 cup vegetable oil (olive or canola)
1 tin (19fl oz.) pure pumpkin
1 cup all purpose flour
2 cups 100% whole-wheat flour
1 tbsp. baking powder
2 tsp. baking soda
2 tsp. ground cinnamon
½ tsp. each ground cloves, ground nutmeg and salt
Finely grated peel of 1 orange
1 cup seedless golden raisins
½ cup unsalted sunflower seeds
½ cup unsalted pumpkin seeds
1/3 cup dark flaxseed

Preheat oven to 350 degrees F or 180 degrees C. Grease two 9 x 5 x 3 inch loaf pans and set aside.

Combine eggs, sugars and oil in a large mixing bowl. Whisk together until blended. Whisk in pumpkin.

In a separate bowl, combine flours, baking powder and soda, seasonings and orange peel. Stir to blend. Gradually stir into pumpkin mixture. Do not over beat.

Fold in remaining ingredients. Divide batter equally between baking pans and smooth the tops.

Bake 60-70 minutes or until a tester inserted in the middle comes out clean. Cool for 10 minutes on a rack, and then remove the cakes and allow them to cool completely. Wrap in plastic. Can be frozen.

DATE NUT BARS

Source: Alive, Canadian Journal of Health and Nutrition #193

2 ½ cups dates, pitted and chopped
2 ½ cups water
½ cup soft tofu, mashed
½ cup organic cold press oil
¾ cup honey
1 tsp. salt
2 cups unbleached white flour
1 ½ cups quick-cooking oats
¾ tsp. baking soda
1 cup chopped nuts (almonds, pecans, or walnuts)

(1 cup of the white flour can be substituted with whole-wheat)

Cook dates and water over low heat until thickened. Beat tofu, oil, honey and salt together in a medium mixing bowl. Add remaining ingredients, one at a time. Press ¾ of the dough into an oiled 9x13 inch pan. Spread the date filling evenly over the dough. Crumble the remaining dough over the dates. Bake at 350 degrees F for 15-20 minutes or until it is slightly browned and the date filling is bubbling. Cool and cut into 24 bars.

Variation: For more flavor, add the juice and zest of 1 large orange or 2 small oranges to the date mixture before you cook it. Reduce the water by the same amount. I also like to add 1 cup raisins.

Note: I have found that letting these bars sit for a week in a refrigerator makes them tastier.

BLUEBERRY BRAN MUFFINS

Source: *Appeal,* (Save-On-Foods) Fall/Winter 1998

1½ cups flour (or 1½ cups whole-wheat flour)

¾ cup All-Bran cereal

1 cup packed brown sugar (or substitute with ¾ cup honey)

2 tsp. baking powder

½ tsp. salt

grated peel of an orange (Peel of two oranges can be used.)

1 cup frozen or fresh blueberries

¼ cup margarine, melted (or use olive or canola oil)

2 tbsp. molasses

1 egg beaten

¼ cup applesauce

1 cup soy beverage

Preheat oven to 375 degrees F. Spray or lightly grease 12 muffin cups.

Combine first 7 ingredients in a large bowl and mix well. Combine remaining ingredients in another bowl and mix well. Add wet ingredients to the dry ones, mixing lightly to combine. Do not over mix. Spoon into prepared muffin cups. Bake about 25 minutes or until an inserted toothpick comes out clean. Cool in pan on rack for fifteen minutes before removing from pan.

Note: If you coat the blueberries in about a tbsp. of flour before you add them to the batter, they will not bleed as much as they would otherwise.

UN-FRIED FRENCH FRIES

Source: *In The Kitchen With Rosie* by Rosie Daley

5 large baking potatoes (about 2 ¾ lbs.)

light vegetable oil cooking spray

2 large egg whites

1 tbsp. Cajun spice

Preheat the oven to 400 degrees F.

Slice each potato lengthwise into ¼ inch ovals, then slice each lengthwise into matchsticks.

Coat a baking sheet with 3 sprays of vegetable oil.

Combine the egg whites and the Cajun spice in a bowl. Add the potatoes and mix to coat. Pour the coated potatoes onto the prepared baking sheet and spread them out into a single layer.

Place the baking sheet on the bottom shelf of the oven. Bake for about 45 minutes, turning every 6-8 minutes until the fries are crispy. Serve immediately.

Note: The same recipe can be used substituting the baking potatoes with **sweet potatoes.**

CARROT-PUMPKIN MUFFINS

Source: *Prevention:* September 1998

1½ cups whole-wheat flour

1½ tsp. pumpkin pie spice

1 tsp. baking soda

½ tsp. baking powder

1 egg or ¼ cup fat-free liquid egg substitute

1 cup canned pumpkin

¾ cup honey

2 tbsp. applesauce

1 tbsp. shredded carrots

Preheat oven to 350 degrees F. Coat a 12-cup muffin tin with nonstick spray. In a large bowl, mix flour, spice, baking soda and baking powder.

In another large bowl, whisk egg, pumpkin, honey, and oil until smooth. Add to flour mixture and stir until combined. Fold in carrots. Spoon into muffin pan. Bake 25 minutes or until an inserted toothpick comes out clean. Remove from pan and cool on a wire rack.

VEGETARIAN CHILI

Source: *Unknown*

1 onion

1 red pepper, chopped

2 garlic cloves, minced

1 celery stalk, chopped

1 tbsp. olive oil

½ tbsp. chili powder

2 tsp. ground cumin

1 can tomatoes (28 oz.)

1 can black or red kidney beans (14 oz.), drained

1 can corn niblets (12 oz.)

1 cup bran cereal

3 cups cooked brown rice

½ cup grated or shredded light cheddar cheese

In a medium pot, cook onion, red pepper, garlic and celery in oil until tender. Stir in chili powder and cumin. Cook 1 minute longer.

Add tomatoes (break up into bite size pieces), beans, corn and cereal. Bring to a boil. Reduce heat, cover and simmer for 5 minutes.

Serve chili in bowls over cooked rice. Sprinkle with cheese if you choose.

Variations: Use 1 tbsp. chili powder and 2x 14 oz. kidney beans. Cook a rice medley of several different kinds of brown rice and wild rice in chicken broth. To serve, the rice can be stirred into the chili mixture or served as suggested above.

BARLEY SALAD WITH TOMATOES AND CORN

Source: *Unknown*

1 cup pearl barley	250 ml
1 cup fresh basil leaves, tightly packed	250 ml
1/3 cup Parmesan cheese, grated	75 ml
¼ cup olive oil	50 ml
½ tsp. each salt and pepper	2 ml
2 cloves garlic, minced	
4 cups cherry tomatoes, halved	1 L
2 cups corn kernels, cooked	500 ml
(About 3 cobs)	

Bring a medium-sized pot of water to boil and add barley.

Reduce heat, cover and simmer. Stir occasionally until tender.

Drain and chill under cold running water.

Puree basil, Parmesan cheese, oil, salt and pepper. Stir in the garlic.

Toss the sauce with the barley. Add tomatoes and corn and toss lightly.

This salad refrigerates well for a couple of days.

Note: I rate my recipes as I use them, and this one was rated "absolutely great".

ROASTED BEETS

Source: *Unknown*

2 lbs. red beets

olive oil

dried basil

salt and pepper

Wash beets and trim stem ends. Place beets on a double tin foil bed, add ¼ cup water and fold into tightly sealed package. Place on a baking sheet in a 425 degrees F oven and bake for one hour or until beets are tender.

Cool, peel and quarter. Place in an oven-proof baking dish. Drizzle with olive oil and sprinkle with basil, salt and pepper. Reheat in a 425 degrees F oven for 15-20 minutes.

EASY KIWI SALAD

Source: *Prevention:* March 1999

6   cups torn Bibb lettuce or baby spinach leaves.

6   kiwifruit, peeled and sliced

4   cans (11oz. each) mandarin oranges, drained or fresh equivalent

1   avocados, peeled, pitted and diced

1   tbsp. honey

2   tsp. walnut oil

¼   cup orange juice

3   tbsp. lime juice

Layer lettuce or spinach, kiwifruit, oranges, and avocadoes on individual plates.

In a small bowl, whisk together honey and oil. Slowly whisk in orange juice and lime juice. Drizzle over salads.

DOUG'S LENTIL SOUP

Source: During a recent trip with friends Judith and Doug, we enjoyed this nutritious and tasty soup that was made by Doug.

1 tbsp. butter and 1 tbsp. olive oil

1 onion, chopped

2 cloves garlic, minced

2 cups carrots, finely diced

1 cup celery, minced

1 cup potatoes, peeled and diced

11/2 cups cooked lentils (cooked from dried or canned)

4 cups chicken or vegetable stock

3 tsp. cumin

salt and pepper to taste

In a large pot, melt the butter over medium heat and add the olive oil. Cook onions, celery, carrots and potatoes for 3 to 4 minutes. Add lentils, stock, and cumin. Add ¼ tsp. salt and 1/8 tsp. pepper. Bring to a boil and simmer over low heat for about 25 minutes or until the vegetables and the lentils are soft. Puree using a food processor or an emersion blender. Add more salt and pepper if needed.

Variations: If you like your soup creamy, add 1 cup skim milk and 2-4 cubes of Havarti cheese before you puree.

Note: Other cheese choices may be provolone, cheddar, or mozzarella.

CLOTHING & ACCESSORIES FOR WOMEN

- ___ swim suit
- ___ undergarments
- ___ slip
- ___ pantyhose
- ___ socks
- ___ scarves
- ___ shoes
- ___ slippers
- ___ shorts & tops
- ___ dress pants
- ___ sweaters
- ___ turtleneck sweater
- ___ rain jacket
- ___ long coat
- ___ skirt, long or short
- ___ warm gloves or mitts
- ___ warm fleece top
- ___ earrings
- ___ visor
- ___ ___
- ___ ___
- ___ ___
- ___ ___
- ___ ___
- ___ ___
- ___ ___

- ___ swim suit
- ___ cover up
- ___ night gown or pajamas
- ___ knee highs
- ___ housecoat
- ___ extra purse
- ___ boots
- ___ runners
- ___ jeans
- ___ blouses
- ___ blazer
- ___ sweat suit
- ___ warm jacket
- ___ dress
- ___ specific sport attire
- ___ sandals
- ___ beach footwear
- ___ neck chains
- ___ hat
- ___ ___
- ___ ___
- ___ ___
- ___ ___
- ___ ___
- ___ ___
- ___ ___

CLOTHING & ACCESSORIES FOR MEN

___ swimming trunks
___ sport socks
___ running shoes
___ dress shoes
___ slippers
___ shorts
___ golf shirts
___ golf slacks
___ specific sports wear
___ dress sports jacket
___ rain wear
___ boots
___ neck scarf
___ chain
___ jeans
___ hat

___ ___
___ ___
___ ___
___ ___
___ ___
___ ___

___ briefs
___ dress socks
___ sandals
___ pajamas
___ robe
___ shirts
___ knit casual tops
___ dress slacks
___ suit
___ long sleeved sweaters
___ warm jacket
___ gloves
___ ties
___ belts
___ cap

___ ___
___ ___
___ ___
___ ___
___ ___
___ ___
___ ___

NON-CLOTHING ITEMS

___ camera
___ spare batteries
___ transformer
___ Swiss army knife
___ matches
___ deck of cards
___ specific sports equipment
___ board games
___ fanny pack
___ flashlight
___ beach towel
___ dental floss
___ lip balm
___ hair dryer
___ shampoo
___ styling gel
___ passports
___ book
___ video camera
___ vitamins
___ motion sickness preparation
___ preparation to stop diarrhea
___ antiseptic cream

___ film
___ battery charger
___ adapters
___ candle
___ umbrella
___ iron
___ crib board
___ CDs
___ money belt
___ sunscreen
___ makeup
___ comb & brush
___ personal phone
___ curling iron
___ conditioner
___ emery boards
___ sunglasses
___ magazine
___ insect repellent
___ supplements
___ laxative
___ painkiller
___ prescription
     medications

___ ____
___ ____
___ ____
___ ____

___ ____
___ ____
___ ____
___ ____

This list can be used for a vacation where you have cooking facilities, usually closer to home.

___ can opener
___ frying pan

___ plastic wrap
___ spices
___ tea, coffee, herb tea
___ canned goods
___ jam
___ cereal

___ eggs
___ bacon
___ vinegar
___ garlic, ginger, onion
___ pancake flour
___ syrup
___ meats
___ fruits
___ pasta

___ ____
___ ____
___ ____
___ ____
___ ____
___ ____
___ ____

___ cork screw
___ plastic storage containers
      (stacking)

___ condiments
___ herbs
___ popcorn
___ toothpicks
___ peanut butter
___ small amounts of
      salt, sugar, flour

___ cheese
___ cooking oil
___ salad dressing
___ bread
___ potatoes
___ milk, yogurt
___ juice
___ vegetables
___ snacks

___ ____
___ ____
___ ____
___ ____
___ ____
___ ____
___ ____

If you would like to suggest an idea that you have successfully used, please share that idea with me at www.planningmeaningfulretirement.com.

Printed in the United States
101687LV00001B/2/P